LANCASH

A GENEALOGICAL BIBLIOGRAPHY

Volume 1

Lancashire Genealogical Sources

by

Stuart A. Raymond

Published by the
Federation of Family History Societies (Publications) Ltd.,
The Benson Room, Birmingham & Midlands Institute,
Margaret Street, Birmingham, B3 3BS, U.K.

Copies also obtainable from:

S.A. & M.J. Raymond, 6, Russet Avenue, Exeter, EX1 3QB, U.K.

First published 1997

Cataloguing in publication data:

Raymond, Stuart A., 1945- . *Lancashire: a genealogical bibliography.* 3 vols.
British genealogical bibliographies. Birmingham: Federation of Family
History Societies, 1996-7. v.1. Lancashire genealogical sources.

DDC: 016.9291094276

ISBN: 1-86006-046-3

ISSN: 1033-2065

Printed and bound by Oxuniprint, Great Clarendon Street, Oxford OX2 6DI

Contents

Introduction

This bibliography is intended primarily for genealogists. It is, however, hoped that it will also prove useful to historians, librarians, archivists, research students, and anyone else interested in the history of Lancashire. It is intended to be used in conjunction with my *English genealogy: an introductory bibliography,* and the other volumes in the *British genealogical bibliographies* series. A full list of these volumes appears on the back cover. This volume lists works on a wide range of subjects of interest to Lancashire genealogists. Volume 2 deals with parish registers and other records of births, marriages, and deaths, monumental inscriptions, and probate records. Pedigrees, family histories, etc., are listed in volume 3.

Many genealogists, when they begin their research, do not realise just how much information has been published, and is readily available in printed form. Not infrequently, they head straight for the archives, rather than checking printed sources first. In so doing, they waste much time, and also impose needless wear and tear on irreplaceable archives. However, when faced with the vast array of tomes possessed by major reference libraries, it is difficult to know where to begin without guidance. This bibliography is intended to point you in the right direction. My aim has been to list everything relating to Lancashire that has been published and is likely to be of use to genealogists. In general, I have not included works which are national in scope but which have local content. Many such works may be identified in *English genealogy: an introductory bibliography,* to which reference is made at appropriate points below. I have also excluded the numerous notes and queries found in family history society and similar journals, except where the content is of importance. Where I have included such notes, replies to them are cited in the form 'see also', with no reference to the names of respondents. Local and church histories are far too numerous to be comprehensively listed, although they frequently provide invaluable information for the genealogist. A select listing of some of the more useful works is given in section 2. This is a bibliography of published works; hence the many manuscript transcripts, *etc.,* to be found in Lancashire libraries are excluded.

Be warned: just because information has been published, it does not necessarily follow that it is accurate. I have not made any judgement on the accuracy of most works listed: that is up to you. If you are able, it is always best to check printed sources against their originals, to determine how accurate the editor was.

Anyone who tries to compile a totally comprehensive bibliography of Lancashire is likely to fall short of his aim. The task is almost impossible, especially if the endeavour is made by one person. That does not, however, mean that the attempt should not be made. This book is intended to be useful to the genealogist: it would fail in that aim if its publication were to be prevented by a vain attempt to ensure total comprehensiveness. I am well aware that there are likely to be omissions – although none, I hope, of books which every Lancashire genealogist should examine. My purpose has primarily been to enable you to identify works which are mostly readily available, and which can be borrowed via the inter-library loan network irrespective of whether you live in London or Melbourne. Most public libraries are able to tap into this network; your local library should be able to borrow most items I have listed, even if it has to go overseas to obtain them.

If you are an assiduous researcher, you may well come across items I have missed. If you do, please let me know, so that they can be included in the next edition.

The work of compiling this bibliography has depended heavily on the resources of the libraries I have used. These included Lancashire County Library's Local Studies Department at Preston, the Harris Library, also at Preston, Lancashire Record Office, Manchester Public Library, Exeter University Library, Exeter City Library, the British Library, and the Society of Genealogists, amongst others. I am grateful to the librarians of all these institutions for their help. Brian Christmas and Rita Hirst both kindly read and commented on early drafts of the book, Mark Gant and Paul Raymond typed the manuscript, and Bob Boyd saw the book through the press. I am grateful too to the officers of the Federation of Family History Societies, whose support is vital for the continuation of this series. My thanks also to my wife Marjorie, and my daughter Mary, who have lived with this book for many months.

Stuart A. Raymond

Abbreviations

B.D.F.H.S.	Bolton and District Family History Society
C.F.H.S.N.	*Cumbria Family History Society newsletter*
C.S.	Chetham Society
C.W.A.A.S.Tr.	*Cumberland & Westmorland Antiquarian & Archaeological Society transactions*
F.H.S.	Family History Society
H.S.L.C.	*Historic Society of Lancashire and Cheshire proceedings/transactions*
L.	*Lancashire [Journal of the L.F.H.H.S.]*
L.C.A.N.	*Lancashire and Cheshire antiquarian notes*
L.C.A.S.	Transactions of the Lancashire and Cheshire Antiquarian Society
L.C.R.S.	Lancashire and Cheshire Record Society
L.F.H.	*Liverpool family historian*
L.F.H.H.S.	Lancashire Family History and Heraldry Society
L.F.H.S.J.	*Liverpool Family History Society journal*
M.G.	*Manchester genealogist*
M.G.H.	*Miscellanea genealogica et heraldica*
M.L.F.H.S.	Manchester & Lancashire Family History Society
N.W.C.H.	*North West catholic history*
N.S.	New series
O.D.F.H.	*Ormskirk and district family historian*
O.S.	Old series
P.N.	*Palatine notebook*
R.S.G.H.[L]	Rossendale Society for Genealogy and Heraldry [Lancashire]

Bibliographic Presentation

Authors' names are in SMALL CAPITALS. Book and journal titles are in *italics*. Articles appearing in journals, and material such as parish register transcripts, forming only part of books are in inverted commas and textface type. Volume numbers are in **bold** and the individual number of the journal may be shown in brackets. These are normally followed by the place of publication (except where this is London, which is omitted), the name of the publisher and the date of publication. In the case of articles, further figures indicate page numbers.

Libraries and Record Offices.

There are many libraries and record offices holding collections relating to Lancashire genealogy; they cannot all be listed here. For a full listing, see:

WYKE, TERRY, & RUDYARD, NIGEL, eds. *Directory of local studies in North West England.* Bibliography of North West England **14**. Manchester: Bibliography of North West England, 1993.

Amongst the most important collections are:

Local Studies Dept.,
Lancashire County Library,
143, Corporation Street,
PRESTON,
Lancashire,
PR1 2UQ

Lancashire Record Office,
Bow Lane,
Preston,
Lancashire,
PR1 2RE

Record Office and Local History Dept.,
Liverpool Libraries and Information Services,
Central Library,
William Brown Street,
Liverpool,
L3 8EW.

Manchester and Lancashire Family History Society,
Clayton House,
59, Piccadilly,
Manchester,
M1 2AQ.

Local Studies Unit,
Manchester Central Library,
St. Peter's Square,
Manchester,
M2 5PD.

1. LANCASHIRE HISTORY

The purpose of genealogy is to trace our ancestral descent, and to place our ancestors within the context of the society in which they lived. These aims cannot be achieved without an appreciation of the historical background. The genealogist ought to read the standard histories of the county/ies in which his forebears lived, and to be aware of the various ways in which the sources used to construct family trees may also be used to recreate the world of the past. For Lancashire, a vast range of historical literature is available, and only a very summary listing can be given here. For further information, consult the bibliographies listed in section 3 below. A number of modern general histories of the county are available:

BAGLEY, J., & HODGKISS, A.G. *A history of Lancashire.* 6th ed. Phillimore, 1976.

FISHWICK, HENRY. *A history of Lancashire.* Elliot Stock, 1894.

FISHWICK, H., & DITCHFIELD, P.H. *Memorials of old Lancashire.* 2 vols. Bemrose & Sons, 1909. Collection of essays.

GOODERSON, P.J. *A history of Lancashire.* B.T. Batsford, 1980.

PHILLIPS, C.B., & SMITH, J.H. *Lancashire and Cheshire from A.D. 1540.* Longman, 1994.

WALTON, JOHN K. *Lancashire: a social history 1558-1939.* Manchester: Manchester University Press, 1987.

County-wide works dealing with specific topics include:

ASHMORE, OWEN. *The industrial archaeology of Lancashire.* Newton Abbot: David & Charles, 1969. Includes a useful bibliography.

ASHMORE, OWEN. *The industrial archaeology of North-West England.* C.S., 3rd series **29**. 1982. Gazetteer covering both Lancashire and Cheshire.

CROSBY, ALAN G., ed. *Lancashire local studies in honour of Diana Winterbotham.* Preston: Carnegie Publishing, 1993. Collection of essays.

FREEMAN, T.W., RODGERS, H.B., & KINVIG, R.H. *Lancashire, Cheshire and the Isle of Man.* Nelson, 1966. Historical geography.

HALLEY, R. *Lancashire: its puritanism and nonconformity.* 2nd ed. Manchester: Tubbs and Brook, 1872. General history of religious life; mentions many names.

MILLWARD, ROY. *Lancashire an illustrated essay on the history of the landscape.* The making of the English landscape **3**. Hodder and Stoughton, 1955.

PEARSON, SARAH. *Rural houses of the Lancashire Pennines, 1560 to 1760.* Royal Comission on Historical Monuments supplementary series **10**. H.M.S.O., 1985.

PEVSNER, NIKOLAUS. *Lancashire.* The buildings of England series. 2 vols. Harmondsworth: Penguin Books, 1969. v.1. The industrial and commercial north. v.2. The rural north.

SHAW, R. CUNLIFFE. *The royal forest of Lancaster.* Preston: [The author], 1956. Extensive, includes separate 'family names index', and many extracts from original sources.

TWYCROSS, EDWARD. *The mansions of England and Wales, illustrated in a series of views of the principal seats, with historical and topographical descriptions: the County Palatine of Lancaster.* 2 vols. Ackermann and Co. 1847. v.1. Hundreds of Blackburn and Leyland. v.2. Hundreds of Lonsdale and Amounderness. Includes limited information on descent.

WALKER, F. *Historical geography of Southwest Lancashire before the industrial revolution.* C.S., N.S., **103**. 1939.

Many older histories of Lancashire were parochial surveys. These are often more directly useful to the genealogist than more modern accounts, since they frequently provide extracts from original sources such as parish registers, monumental inscriptions, *etc.,* they also often include pedigrees. See:

AIKIN, J. *A description of the country from thirty to forty miles around Manchester ...* John Stockdale, 1795. Reprinted Newton Abbot: David & Charles, 1968.

BAINES, EDWARD. *History of the County Palatine and Duchy of Lancaster.* 4 vols. Fisher Son & Co., 1836. See also the new edition, ed. James Croston. 5 vols. Manchester: John Heywood, 1888. Probably the most important parochial survey; includes many pedigrees, lists of clergy, biographical notices, *etc., etc.* There is also an edition of 1868-70, which excludes the pedigrees.

CORRY, J. *The history of Lancashire.* 2 vols. Geo. B. Whittaker, 1825. Primarily a parochial survey, with notes on descent and a few pedigrees, *etc.* .

GASTRELL, FRANCIS. *Notitia Cestriensis, or historical notices of the Diocese of Chester,* ed. F.R. Raines. C.S., O.S. 19 & 21-2. 1849-50. Vol. 2. Lancashire.

GREGSON, MATTHEW. *Portfolio of fragments, relative to the history and antiquities, topography and genealogies of the County Palatine and Duchy of Lancaster.* 3rd ed., ed. John Harland. George Routledge and Sons, 1869. Parochial survey, with many extracts from original sources.

There are numerous works dealing with particular periods. The list which follows is very selective, and is biased towards general works based on sources of interest to genealogists. For ease of reference, the listing is arranged by period.

Medieval, to 1500

AULT, WARREN ORTMAN. *Private jurisdiction in England.* New Haven: Yale University Press. 1923. Includes chapters on the medieval courts of the Honor of Clitheroe, the Barony of Furness and the Barony of Manchester, including extracts from court records *etc.*

BENNETT, MICHAEL J. *Community, class and careerism: Cheshire and Lancashire society in the age of Sir Gawain and the Green Knight.* Cambridge: Cambridge University Press, 1983. Important.

SOMERVILLE, R. 'The Duchy and County Palatine of Lancaster' *H.S.L.C.* 103, 1951, 59-67. General account, medieval.

WALKER, S.K. 'Lordship and lawlessness in the Palatinate of Lancaster, 1370-1400', *Journal of British studies* 28, 1989, 325-48.

Early Modern, 1500-1800

HAIGH, CHRISTOPHER. *Reformation and resistance in Tudor Lancashire.* Cambridge: Cambridge University Press, 1975. Includes good bibliography.

JORDAN, W.K. *The social institutions of Lancashire: a study of the changing patterns of aspirations in Lancashire, 1480-1660.* C.S., 3rd Series 11. 1962. Based on wills.

HOYLE, R.W. 'Resistance and manipulation in early Tudor taxation: some evidence from the North', *Archives* 20(90), 1993, 158-76. Based on Lancashire subsidy returns, early 16th c.

LOWE, NORMAN. *The Lancashire textile industry in the sixteenth century.* C.S., 3rd series 20. 1972. Includes a few probate inventories.

ASHMORE, OWEN. 'Household inventories of the Lancashire gentry, 1550-1700', *H.S.L.C.* 110, 1958, 59-105. Wide-ranging discussion of their contents, with list of probate records used.

HOLLINSHEAD, J.E. 'The gentry of South-West Lancashire in the later sixteenth century', *Northern history* 26, 1990, 82-102. Includes list of probate inventories for the gentry of Childwall, Huyton, Prescot and Walton.

LANGTON, JOHN. *Geographical change and industrial revolution: coalmining in South West Lancashire, 1590-1799.* Cambridge: C.U.P., 1979. Includes bibliography.

ADDY, JOHN. *Sin and society in the seventeenth century.* Routledge, 1989. Based on cause papers in the Chester Diocesan archives.

WADSWORTH, ALFRED P., & MANN, JULIA DE LACY. *The cotton trade and industrial Lancashire, 1600-1780.* Manchester University Press, 1931.

ROGERS, C.D. *The Lancashire population crisis of 1623.* Manchester: Manchester University Extra Mural Department, 1975. Based on parish registers.

BLACKWOOD, B.G. 'The economic state of the Lancashire gentry on the eve of the Civil War', *Northern history* 12, 1976, 53-83.

CARTER, D.P. 'The exact militia in Lancashire, 1625-1640', *Northern history* 11, 1976 for 1975, 87-106.

BLACKWOOD, B.G. *The Lancashire gentry and the Great Rebellion, 1640-60.* C.S., 3rd series 25. 1978. Reviewed in MORRILL, J.S. 'The Northern gentry and the Great Rebellion', *Northern history* 15, 1978, 66-87.

BROXAP, ERNEST. *The great civil war in Lancashire (1642-1651).* 2nd ed. Manchester: Manchester University Press, 1973.

BLACKWOOD, B.G. 'Parties and issues in the Civil War in Lancashire and East Anglia', *Northern history* 29, 1993, 99-125. i.e. Norfolk and Suffolk.

BLACKWOOD, B.G. 'The Cavalier and Roundhead gentry of Lancashire', *L.C.A.S.* 77, 1967, 77-96.

BLACKWOOD, B.G. 'The catholic and protestant gentry of Lancashire during the Civil War period', *H.S.L.C.* 126, 1975, 1-29.

FESSLER, ALFRED. 'The official attitude towards the sick poor in seventeenth-century Lancashire', *H.S.L.C.* 102, 1956, 85-113.

HAIGH, C.A. 'Slander and the church courts in the sixteenth century', *L.C.A.S.* 78, 1975, 1-13. Based on records of the Consistory Court of the Bishop of Chester.

FRANCE, R. SHARPE 'A history of plague in Lancashire', *H.S.L.C.* 90, 1938, 1-175. Includes transcript of a plague rate levied in Salford Hundred, 1605; list of those infected in Salford Hundred, 1605; list of those infected in Ormskirk 1653; list of farmers who lost cattle from cattle plague in Lonsdale, 1749-50.

HOWSON, W.G. 'Plague, poverty and population in parts of North-West England', *H.S.L.C.* 112, 1960, 29-55. Based on published parish registers.

LANGTON, J. 'Landowners and the development of coal mining in South-West Lancashire, 1590-1799', in FOX, H.S.A., & BUTLIN, R.A., eds. *Change in the countryside: essays on rural England 1500-1900.* Special publication 10. Institute of British Geographers, 1979, 123-44

RILEY, D. 'Wealth and social structure in north-western Lancashire in the later seventeenth-century: a new use for probate inventories', *H.S.L.C.* 141, 1992, 77-100. Study of appraisers.

SWAIN, JOHN T. *Industry before the industrial revolution: North-East Lancashire, c.1500-1640.* C.S., 3rd series, 32. 1986.

Nineteenth-Century

ANDERSON, B.L., & STONEY, P.J.M., eds. *Commerce, industry and transport: studies in economic change on Merseyside.* Liverpool: Liverpool University Press, 1983. Collection of essays, 18-20th c.

ANDERSON, MICHAEL. *Family structure in nineteenth century Lancashire.* Cambridge studies in sociology 5. Cambridge: Cambridge University Press, 1971. General study, mainly based on census data, 1841-61.

SANDERSON, MICHAEL. 'Social change and elementary education in industrial Lancashire, 1789-1840', *Northern history* 3, 1968, 131-54.

BELCHEM, JOHN., ed. *Popular politics, riot and labour: essays in Liverpool history, 1790-1940.* Liverpool: Liverpool University Press, 1972.

BELL, S.P., ed. *Victorian Lancashire.* Newton Abbot: David & Charles, 1974.

BOHSTEDT, JOHN. *Riots and community politics in England and Wales, 1790-1810.* Cambridge, Massachusetts: Harvard University Press, 1983. Includes chapters on the Lancashire weavers, and on Manchester.

CHAPMAN, SYDNEY J. *The Lancashire cotton industry, a study in economic development.* Manchester: University Press, 1904. 18-19th c.

COLLIER, FRANCES. *The family economy of the working classes in the cotton industry 1784-1833,* ed. R.S. Fitton. C.S., 3rd series 12. 1965.

EVANS, ERIC J. 'Landownership and the exercise of power in an industrialising society: Lancashire and Cheshire in the nineteenth century', in GIBSON, RALPH, & BLINKHORN, MARTIN, eds. *Landownership and power in modern Europe.* Harper Collins, 1991, 145-63.

FOSTER, D. 'Class and county government in early nineteenth-century Lancashire', *Northern history* **9**, 1974, 48-61.

FOSTER, D. 'The politics of uncontested elections: North Lancashire 1832-1865', *Northern history* **13**, 1977, 232-47.

GREGORY, D. 'Rates and representation: Lancashire county in the nineteenth century', *Northern history* **12**, 1976, 158-71.

LAWTON, R. 'Population trends in Lancashire and Cheshire from 1801', *H.S.L.C.* **114**, 1962, 189-213. Based on the census.

LONGMATE, NORMAN. *The hungry mills.* Temple Smith, 1978. The story of the Lancashire cotton famine, 1861-5.

MIDWINTER, ERIC. *Social administration in Lancashire 1830-1860: poor law, public health, and policies.* Manchester: Manchester University Press, 1969. Includes list of primary sources used.

MUTCH, A. 'The 'farming ladder' in North Lancashire, 1840-1914: myth or reality', *Northern history* **27**, 1991, 162-83. Questions whether farm servants progressed to small farm ownership.

ROGERS, G. 'Lancashire landowners and the great agricultural depression', *Northern history* **22**, 1986, 250-68.

SMELSER, NEIL J. *Social change in the Industrial Revolution: an application of theory to the Lancashire cotton industry, 1770-1840.* Routledge & Kegan Paul, 1959. Includes extensive bibliography listing many Parliamentary papers.

WALLER, P.J. *Democracy and sectarianism: a political and social history of Liverpool, 1868-1939.* Liverpool: Liverpool University Press, 1981. Includes biographical dictionary of prominent people.

DAVIES, ANDREW. *Leisure, gender and poverty: working-class culture in Salford and Manchester, 1900-1939.* Buckingham: Open University, 1992.

2. PARISH, TOWNSHIP AND LOCAL HISTORIES

There are innumerable histories of particular places in Lancashire; a full listing is well beyond the scope of the present work. This listing attempts to identify those works which have a particular value to genealogists — works which either include substantial extracts from original sources, or which have a wider importance than the merely local.

Accrington
AINSWORTH, RICHARD. *The old homesteads of Accrington and district.* Accrington: Wardleworth, 1928. Gives descents of many properties.

TURNER, WILLIAM. 'Patterns of migration of textile workers into Accrington in the early nineteenth century', *Local population studies* **30**, 1983, 28-34.

See also Rossendale

Ainsdale
See Birkdale

Allerton
STEWART-BROWN, RONALD. *A history of the manor and township of Allerton in the county of Lancaster.* Liverpool: E. Howell, 1911. Includes much information on the descent of the manor.

Arkholme
CHIPPINDALL, W.H. 'The history of the township of Arkholme in the county of Lancaster', *Chetham miscellanies* N.S., **90**, 1931, separately paginated. Many descents of properties. Includes pedigrees (some folded) of Storrs, Smith, Cort, Barker and Withers.

Ashton under Lyne
BOWMAN, WINIFRED. *England in Ashton-under-Lyne, being the history of the whole ancient manor and parish, including Ashton Town, Alt, Alt Edge, Audenshaw, Bardsley, Crossbank, Hooley Hill, Hurst, Limehurst (with Waterloo), Lees, Littlemoss, Luzley, Mossley,*

Smallshaw, Stalybridge (Lancashire side), Taunton, Waterhouses, Woodhouses and Wood Park. Ashton under Lyne: John Sherratt and Son, 1960. Extensive; includes manorial descent, an 'order of seating', 1422, biographical notes on clergy, extracts from overseers' accounts 1718, assessment of 1618, list of mayors, a good bibliography, *etc., etc.*

GLOVER, WILLIAM. *History of Ashton under Lyne and the surrounding district,* ed. John Andrew. Ashton under Lyne: J.Andrew & Co., 1881. Includes chapter on the Assheton familly, also subsidy roll for 1618, and rent roll, 1422.

Atherton
LUNN, J. *History of Atherton.* Atherton: Atherton District Council, 1971. Includes many lists of names, e.g. the protestation return, 1641/2, list of principal inhabitants 1792, extract from Baines *directory* 1824, *etc.*

Aughton
NEWSTEAD, G. COULTHARD. *Gleanings towards the annals of Aughton, near Ormskirk.* Liverpool: C.H. Ratcliffe, 1893. Includes list of rectors, and much information on parish registers, churchwardens' accounts, constables' accounts, waywardens' accounts, *etc.*

Barrow in Furness
SAUNDERS, MARK N.K. 'Migration to 19th century Barrow in Furness: an examination of the census enumerators' books, 1841-1871', *C.W.A.A.S.Tr.* N.S. **84**, 1984 21525.

Billington
ABRAM, WILLIAM ALEXANDER. 'A history of the township of Billington, in the parish of Blackburn, Co. Lancaster: its ancient families, lords and freeholders, with an account of the parochial chapel and chapelry of Langho', *H.S.L.C.,* **25**, N.S., **13**, 1873, 153-236. Includes many descents, also 1539 survey, list of tenants, 1872, *etc.*

Birch
BOOKER, JOHN. *The history of the ancient chapel of Birch, in Manchester parish, including a sketch of the township of Rusholme ... together with notices of the more ancient local families and particulars relating to the descent of their estates.* C.S., O.S., **47**. 1859. Includes many deeds of the Trafford, Rusholme, Platt and Birch families, with pedigrees of Worsley, 17-19th c., Platt, 13-17th c., Edge, 17th c., Siddall, 16-18th c., Dickenson, 18-19th c., also chapel seating plan of 1640.

Birkdale
HARROP, SYLVIA, ed. *Families and cottages of old Birkdale and Ainsdale.* Preston: Carnegie Publishing, 1992. Includes various pedigrees.

Bispham
FISHWICK, HENRY. *The history of the parish of Bispham in the county of Lancaster.* C.S., N.S., **10**, 1887. Includes protestation return, 1641/2, monumental inscriptions, notes on curates, pedigrees (some folded), of Veale, Rigby, and Bamber, wills, 16-17th c., *etc.*

Blackburn
ABRAM, M. ALEXANDER. *Parish of Blackburn, County of Lancaster: a history of Blackburn town and parish.* Blackburn: J.G. & J.Toulmin, 1877. Second book arranged by township; includes much biographical information.

BEATTIE, DEREK. *Blackburn: the development of a Lancashire cotton town.* Keele: Ryburn Publishing, 1992.

WHITTLE, P.A. *Blackburn as it is: a topographical, statistical and historical account ...* Preston: H.Oakey, 1852. Includes 'biographical sketches of eminent men' and a directory for 1852.

Blackburnshire
SMITH, R.B. *Blackburnshire: a study in early Lancashire history.* Dept. of English Local History occasional papers **15**. Leicester: University of Leicester, 1961. 14th c. study.

Blackley

BOOKER, JOHN. *A history of the ancient chapel of Blackley in Manchester parish, including sketches of the townships of Blackley, Harpurhey, Moston and Crumpsall ... together with notices of the more ancient local families and particulars relating to the descent of their estates.* Manchester: George Simms, 1854. Includes pedigrees, extracts from the parish registers, inscriptions, *etc.*

Bolton

DYER, ALAN. 'Epidemics of measles in a seventeenth-century English town', *Local population studies* **34**, 1985, 35-45. Based on Bolton parish registers.

Briercliffe

FROST, R.B. 'Probate inventories: what they reveal about Briercliffe in the eighteenth century', *Lancaster local historian* **2**, 1984, 23-7. Brief.

Burnage

See Didsbury

Bury

GRAY, MARGARET. *The history of Bury, Lancashire, from 1660-1876.* Bury: Bury Times, 1970. Includes much information from wills and poor law records, *etc.*

Cartmel

KIRBY, R.H., et al, eds. *The rural deanery of Cartmel in the diocese of Carlisle: its churches and monuments.* Ulverston: James Atkinson, 1892. A parochial survey, including notes on monuments, lists of incumbents, etc., with many names.

STOCKDALE, JAMES. *Annales Caermoelenses, or, annals of Cartmel.* Ulverston: William Kitchin, 1872. Includes many extracts from original sources, e.g. parish registers, wills, enclosure awards, *etc.*

See also Furness

Chipping

SMITH, TOM C. *History of the parish of Chipping, in the county of Lancaster, with some account of the forests of Bleasdale and Bowland.* Preston: C.W.

Whitehead, 1894. Extensive; includes baptisms, 1559-84, and marriages, 1599-1635, plus a few burials and later extracts; also pedigrees of Parkinson, Knoll, Sherborne, Swinglehurst and Eccles, and notes on many other families, *etc., etc.*

IRONFIELD, CHRISTINE. 'The parish of Chipping during the seventeenth century', *H.S.L.C.* **127**, 1978, 25-46. Based on probate records, hearth tax returns, and estate records, *etc.*

Chorlton

See Didsbury

Claughton

See Over Kellett

Clayton le Moors

TRAPPES-LOMAX, RICHARD. *A history of the township and manor of Clayton le Moors, Co. Lancaster.* C.S., N.S., **85**. 1926. Includes pedigrees (some folded) of Clayton, Grimshaw, Lomax, Whalley, Rishton, Dunkenhalgh, Duxbury, etc.

Clitheroe

MULLETT, M.A. 'Men of knowne loyalty: the politics of the Lancashire borough of Clitheroe, 1660-1689', *Northern history* **21**, 1985, 108-36.

WEEKS, WILLIAM SELF. *Clitheroe in the seventeenth century, illustrated by copious extracts from the Clitheroe borough records and other unpublished local documents.* 2 vols. Clitheroe: Clitheroe Advertiser & Times, 1927.

WEEKS, WILLIAM SELF. *The Clitheroe parish church bells.* Clitheroe: Advertiser & Times, [189-?]

Crumpsall

See Blackley

Darwen

TAYLOR, W.J. 'A Lancashire township, 3: Darwen', *L.* **7**(2), 1986, 30-40. Many names mentioned.

Davyhulme

See Flixton

Didsbury

BOOKER, JOHN. *A history of the ancient chapels of Didsbury and Chorlton, in the Manchester parish, including sketches of the townships of Didsbury, Withington, Burnage, Heaton Norris, Reddish, Levenshulme, and Chorlton-cum-Hardy, together with notices of more ancient local families, and particulars relating to the descent of their estates.* C.S., O.S., **42**. 1857. Includes extracts from Didsbury parish registers 1562-1856, chapelwardens accounts 1645-1746, pedigrees of Longford, Mosley, Reddish, Barlow, and Hulme, *etc.*

Dob Lane
See Newton

Failsworth
See Newton

Flixton

LANGTON, DAVID HERBERT. *A history of the parish of Flixton (Lancashire), comprising the townships of Flixton and Urmston, with a short sketch of the adjoining hamlet of Davyhulme.* Manchester: Taylor, Garnett, Evans & Co., 1898. Includes list of clergy, extracts from parish register and churchwardens accounts *etc.*

LAWSON, RICHARD. *History of Flixton, Urmston and Davyhulme.* Urmston: Richard Lawson, 1898. Includes monumental inscription, constables accounts, early 19th c., protestation return, 1641/2, *etc.*

LEECH, DANIEL JOHN. 'Flixton and its church', *L.C.A.S.,* **4**, 1886, 182-98. Mainly descents of properties, also includes extracts from the parish register relating to Radcliffe, Asshawe, and Egerton.

Formby

WEBB, N.C. 'Poverty and the poor law in Formby 1701-1900', *Lancashire local historian* **9**, 1994 12-19. Brief general study.

Furness

MARSHALL, J.D. *Furness and the industrial revolution: an economic history of Furness (1711-1900) and the town of Barrow (1757-1897) with an epilogue.* Barrow in Furness: Barrow in Furness Library and Museum Commitee, 1958.

WEST, THOMAS. *The antiquities of Furness.* New ed. Ulverston: George Ashburner, 1813. Focuses on the abbey and important local families; includes survey of 1649.

BARBER, HENRY. *Furness and Cartmel notes, or, jottings of topographical, ecclesiastical and popular antiquities, and of historical circumstances, as well as interesting facts relating to the districts of Furness and Cartmel.* Ulverston: James Atkinson, 1894. Includes list of Furness family names, survey of church lands, 1649, *etc.*

WHELLAN, WILLIAM. *The history and topography of the counties of Cumberland and Westmorland, with Furness and Cartmel in Lancashire ...* Pontefract: W Whelton & Co., 1860. A major parochial survey, with lists of M.P's, clergy, *etc,* and many genealogical notes.

Fylde

PORTER, JOHN. *History of the Fylde of Lancashire.* Fleetwood: W. Porter & Sons, 1876. Reprinted East Ardsley: S.R.Publishers, 1968. Includes parochial survey.

Garstang

FISHWICK, HENRY. *History of the parish of Garstang in the county of Lancaster.* C.S., O.S., **104-5**. 1878-9. Includes rental, 1604/5, extracts from parish register, 1567-1676, extensive biographical notes on vicars, and many property descents, including pedigrees (some folded) of Rigmayden, Fyfe, Plesington, Catterall, Brockholes, Whitehead and Cottam, with protestation return, 1641/2.

Goosnargh

FISHWICK, HENRY. *The history of the parochial chapel of Goosnargh, in the county of Lancaster.* Manchester: Charles Simms and Co., 1871. Includes biographical notes on clergy, extracts from the records of the 'sworn men', list of churchwardens, notes on many families, with pedigrees, extracts from parish registers, monumental inscriptions, list of persons liable to pay taxes 1671, *etc., etc.*

Gressingham

CHIPPINDALL, W.H. *History of the township of Gressingham.* Kendal: Atkinson & Pollitt, 1919. Includes much information on local families, including folded pedigrees of Chippindale, Dickson or Dixon, Borwick, Burton, Higham and Denny.
See also Over Kellett

Harpurhey
See Blackley

Haslingden

TODD, ANDREW A. 'A Lancashire township, 1: Haslingden', *L.* **6**(3), 1985, 3033. Includes extracts from registers, *etc.*
WOODCOCK, THOMAS. *Haslingden: a topographical history.* C.S. 3rd series. **4**, 1952. Includes rental, 1766, various deeds, property descents, notes on the Holden family, *etc.*
See also Rossendale

Hawkshead

OOSTERVEN, KARLA. 'Hawkshead (Lancs) mobility (geographical and occupational) as shown by the reconstitution of the parish from the registers, 1585-1840', *Local population studies* **12**, 1974, 38-41.

Heaton Norris
See Didsbury

Holcombe

DOWSETT, H *Holcombe long ago.* Holcombe: Litle Holcombe Books, 1988. Originally published 1902. Includes lists of clergy, sidesmen and churchwardens, with extracts from parish registers, *etc.*

Ireby

CHIPPINDALL, W.H. *History of the township of Ireby.* C.S., N.S., **95**. 1935. Includes numerous pedigrees, inquisitions post mortem, wills, *etc.* Primarily descents of properties.

Kirkham

FISHWICK, HENRY. *The history of the parish of Kirkham, in the county of Lancaster.* C.S., O.S., **92**. 1874. Includes parish register, 1539-1620, monumental inscriptions, many extracts from parish records, biographical notes on masters of the grammar school and pedigrees (some folded) of Westby, Bradkirk, Parker, Harrison, Skillicorne, Leyland, Hesketh, Ffrance and Sharples, *etc.*
SHAW, R. CUNLIFFE. *Kirkham in Amounderness: the story of a Lancashire community.* 2nd ed. Preston: R. Seed & Sons, 1949. Extensive; includes many extracts from manorial records, with pedigrees of Kirkham, Bradkirk, Cottam, Browne, Loxham, Langton, Birley, Hornby and Shaw.

Kirkmanshulme
See Newton

Lancaster

MULLETT, M A. 'Conflict, politics and elections in Lancaster 1660-1688', *Northern history* **19**, 1983, 61-86.
MOORHOUSE, LINDA *The good old town of Lancaster in 1841.* [Lancaster]: [ ], [1995]. Includes marriages and deaths notices from newspapers.

Levenshulme
See Didsbury

Lytham

FISHWICK, HENRY. *The history of the parish of Lytham in the county of Lancaster.* C.S., N.S., **60**, 1907. Includes lay subsidy rolls, 1545-6 and 1640/41, list of 'contributors' to the 'free and voluntary present', 1661, list of inhabitants, 1676, monumental inscriptions, notes on clergy, *etc.*

Liverpool

HARRIS, J.R., ed. *Liverpool and Merseyside: essays on the economic and social history of the port and its hinterland.* Frank Cass & Co., 1969. Collection of essays, some of which are listed elsewhere in this bibliography.
MUIR, JOHN RAMSEY BRYCE. *A history of Liverpool.* Liverpool: University Press, 1907. Includes a useful 'Appendix: note on authorities'.

POOLEY, COLIN G. 'The residential segregation of migrant communities in mid-Victorian Liverpool', *The Institute of British Geographers transactions* N.S., **2**, 1977, 364-82. Based on the 1871 census.

Longridge
SMITH, T.M.C. *A history of Longridge and district.* Preston: C.W. Whitehead, 1888. Includes pedigrees of Hothersall, Townley, Cave, etc., with biographical notes on clergy and other notables, *etc.*

Loveclough
ASPDEN, ROY. 'Families of Loveclough, 1507-1660', *L.* **11**(1), 1990, 16-21.

Manchester
AXON, W E.A. *The annals of Manchester: a chronological record from the earliest times to the end of 1885.* John Heywood, 1886. Innumerable names; records many deaths.

FRANGOPULO, N J., ed. *Rich inheritance: a guide to the history of Manchester.* Manchester: Manchester Education Committee, 1962. General study.

HARLAND, JOHN. *Mamecestre: being chapters from the early recorded history of the Baronry, the lordship or manor, the vill, borough, or town, of Manchester.* C.S., O.S., **53, 56,** & **58**. 1861-2. Includes survey of the manor of Manchester, 1320, extent, 1322, rental, 1473, and many other medieval documents, with various descents, *etc.*

KIDD, A AN. *Manchester.* Town and city histories. Keele: Ryburn Publishing, 1993.

LLOYD-JONES, ROGER, & LEWIS, M J. *Manchester and the age of the factory: the business structure of cottonopolis in the industrial revolution.* Beckenham: Croom Helm, 1988. Early 19th c., includes bibliography.

TAIT, JAMES. *Medieval Manchester and the beginnings of Lancashire.* Manchester: Manchester University Press, 1904. Reprinted Didsbury: E.J. Morten, 1972. Scholarly; includes chapter on the Grelley family.

WILLAN, T S. *Elizabethan Manchester.* C.S., 3rd series. **27**, 1980. Includes rental, 1599-1600, and list of probate inventories, 1570-1602.

WILLAN, T S. 'Plague in perspective: the case of Manchester in 1605', *H.S.L.C.* **132**, 1983, 29-40. Based on parish registers.

BOOT, H M. 'Unemployment and poor law relief in Manchester, 1845-1850', *Social history* **15**, 1990, 217-28. General study.

Moston
See Blackley

Newton
CROFTON, H T. *A history of Newton chapelry in the ancient parish of Manchester, including sketches of the township of Newton with Kirkmanshulme, Failsworth and Bradford, but exclusive of the townships of Droylsden and Moston, together with the notices of local families and persons.* C.S., N.S., **52-5.** 1904-5. Includes index to baptisms at Newton chapel, 1656-1700, other extracts from the registers, list of wills, protestation return 1641/2, pedigrees of Armitage, Chetham, Smith and Beswick, abstracts of manorial records, chapel rates, 1755, 1819 and 1837, index of Dob Lane chapel register (nonconformist), lists of Failsworth wills and overseers, *etc., etc.*

North Meols
FARRER, WILLIAM. *A history of the parish of North Meols, in the Hundred of West Derby and County of Lancaster ...* Liverpool: Henry Young and Sons, 1903. Includes manorial descent, list of clergy, monumental inscriptions, folded pedigrees of Coudray, Aughton and Hesketh families, 13-19th c., *etc.*

Oldham
BUCKLEY, A.D. 'Oldham: the population and social structure of a Lancashire parish on the eve of the Civil War', *M.G.* **27**(2), 1991, 16-19; **27**(3), 1991, 23-8; **27**(4), 1991, 12-16.

Over Kellett

LOSCHSKY, D.J., & KERR, D.F. 'Income and family size in three Lancashire parishes: a reconstitution study', *Journal of economic history* 29(3), 1969, 429-48. Based on the parish registers of Over Kellett, Gressingham and Claughton.

Pendle

BRIGG, MARY. 'The Forest of Pendle in the seventeenth century', *H.S.L.C.* 113, 1961, 65-96; 115, 1963, 65-90. Based on probate records.

Pennington

FELL, ALFRED. *A Furness manor: Pennington and its church.* Ulverston: Kitchin & Co., 1929. Includes manorial descent, notes on the parish register, list of clergy, *etc.*

Poulton le Fylde

FISHWICK, HENRY. *The history of the parish of Poulton-le-Fylde in the county of Lancaster.* C.S., N.S., 8. 1885. Includes monumental inscriptions, notes on clergy, extracts from the parish register, 1591-1692, protestation return, 1641/2, pedigrees of Singleton and Allan, wills, 16th c., tax assessments of 1660 and 1702, *etc.*

Preston

CLEMESHA, H.W. *A history of Preston in Amounderness.* Manchester: University Press, 1912. Substantial general history, includes list of clergy.

FISHWICK, HENRY. *The history of the parish of Preston in Amounderness in the county of Lancaster.* Rochdale: James Clegg, 1900. Extensive; includes lists of mayors and clergy, notes on, and pedigrees of, many families, the protestation return, 1641/2, hearth tax return, 1663, *etc.*

Prestwich

BOOKER, JOHN. *Memorials of the church in Prestwich, being a contribution towards the history of the parent church of the parish, including notices of the local families, their pedigrees, etc., extracts from the parish register and records,* *illustrating the descent of families adjacent and remote, constituting, in a certain degree, the history of the place, derived chiefly from unpublished and authentic sources.* Manchester: Simms and Dunham, 1852.

Reddish

See Didsbury

Ribchester

SMITH, T.M.C., & SHORTT, J.NATHAN. *The history of the parish of Ribchester, in the county of Lancaster.* Bemrose & Sons, 1890. Includes list of clergy and churchwardens, transcript of the parish register, 1598-1812, monumental inscriptions, notes on many families, *etc.*

Rochdale

FISHWICK, HENRY. *The history of the parish of Rochdale, in the county of Lancaster.* Rochdale: James Clegg, 1889. Includes biographical notes on clergy, notes on many families, the 1641/2 protestation return, *etc.*

Rossendale

NEWBIGGING, THOMAS. *History of the forest of Rossendale.* 2nd ed. Rawtenstall: J.J. Riley, 1893. Includes list of 'Graves', i.e. forest officers, 1559-1818, list of overseers, 1681-1790, muster roll 1553, *etc., etc.*

TUPLING, G.H. *The economic history of Rossendale.* C.S., N.S., 86. 1927. Includes list of Accrington copyholders, 1543-67, list of Haslingden tenants' encroachments, 1616, list of leases granted in Accrington 1579-91, Haslingden rental, 1600, Haslingden enclosure award, 1618, *etc.* Important general study.

Saint Michael on Wyre

FISHWICK, HENRY. *The history of the parish of St. Michaels-on-Wyre in the county of Lancaster, with an appendix containing a transcript of the registers of the chapelry of Woodplumpton for 1604 to 1613.* C.S., N.S., 25. 1891. Includes protestation return 1641/2, list of recusants, 1610, lay subsidy returns of 1332 and 16th c., rent roll, 1451, monumental inscriptions, biographical notes on clergy, pedigrees of Butler, Kirksby, Kighly, Stanley, Ambrose and Leckonby (some folded), transcript of Woodplumpton chapel registers 1604-13, wills, *etc.*

Sefton

WILLIAMS, THOMAS. 'Some events and personalities concerned with the parish of Sefton and the Free Grammar School (Merchant Taylor's) at Great Crosby, 1755-1811', *H.S.L.C.* **104**, 1952, 117-41. General account.

Stretford

CROFTON, H.T. *A history of the ancient chapel of Stretford in Manchester parish, including sketches of the township of Stretford together with notices of local families and persons.* C.S., N.S., **42, 45,** and **51.** 1899-1903. Includes extensive extracts from the parish register, 1598-1813, monumental inscriptions, list of wills, notes on clergy, extracts from churchwardens' accounts and manorial records, extracts from 1782 survey, pedigree of Trafford, medieval-19th c., *etc.*

Thornton

PRIESTLEY, KAY. 'A Lancashire township: 2: Thornton', *L.* **7**(1), 1986, 19 & 226. Includes land tax assesment, 1798-9, tithe appointment 1840, and many other names.

Tunstall

CHIPPINDALL, W.H. *A history of the parish of Tunstall.* C.S., N.S., **104.** 1940. Includes lay subsidies, 1543, 1625/6, and 1628/9, enclosure award, 1825, monumental inscriptions, and many pedigrees and descents.

Urmston

See Flixton

Warton

LUCAS, JOHN. *John Lucas's history of Warton Parish (compiled 1710-1740),* ed. J. Rawlinson Ford & J.A. Fuller-Maitland. Kendal: Titus Wilson & Son, 1831. Includes extensive list of recusants, 1629-32.

SPEAKE, R 'The historical demography of Warton parish before 1801', *H.S.L.C.,* **122,** 1970, 43-65. Based on parish registers.

Whalley

WHITAKER, THOMAS D. *A history of the original parish of Whalley and the honour of Clitheroe, to which is subjoined an account of the parish of Cartmell.* 4th ed. revised by John Gough Nichols & Ponsonby A. Lyons. 2 vols. George Routledge and Sons, 1872-6. Includes many pedigrees, extracts from original sources, biographical memoirs, list of clergy, *etc,* also chapters on Blackburn and Rochdale.

Whittington

CHIPPINDALL, W.H. *A history of Whittington.* C.S., N.S., **99.** 1938. Includes list of tenants, 1654, list of landowners, 1848, lay subsidies, 1625/6, 1640/41, will abstracts, various pedigrees and descents, list of rectors, monumental inscriptions, *etc.*

Wigan

SINCLAIR, DAVID. *The history of Wigan.* 2 vols. Wigan: Wall, 1882. Includes pollbook for 1640, burgess list, 1649, extracts from court rolls, 17-18th c., *etc., etc.*

Wittington

See Didsbury

Woodplumpton

See Saint Michael on Wyre

3. BIBLIOGRAPHY AND ARCHIVES

A. General

Lancashire has a bewildering array of libraries, record offices, genealogical and historical societies, and museums. Fortunately, a detailed and indispensable guide to these institutions is available:

WYKE, TERRY, & RUDYARD, NIGEL. *Directory of local studies in North West England. Bibliography of North West England* 14. 1993.

See also:

MANCHESTER & LANCASHIRE FAMILY HISTORY SOCIETY. *Handbook: a guide to genealogical sources.* 3rd ed. Manchester: the Society, 1993. Brief summary; more general than local.

MASON, MARNIE. 'The Manchester and Lancashire Family History Society', *Manchester region history review* 3(2), 1989/90, 436.

Genealogists handbook of South West Lancashire. Liverpool: Liverpool & S.W. Lancashire F.H.S., 1991. Includes notes on repositories, list of local registers, maps, *etc.*

Local studies in Lancashire: a guide to resources. [Preston]: Lancashire Library, 1986. Guide to holdings in the libraries of Lancashire County Council.

The various institutions listed in these works house a vast array of printed and archival material. Published works on Lancashire history are innumerable; the best guides to them are the volumes in the *Lancashire bibliography* series. Some of these, however, are now rather dated. The relevant 'period' volumes are as follows:

HORROCKS, SIDNEY, ed. *Lancashire history: historical periods Norman, Plantagenet, Lancaster & York, Tudor.* A contribution towards a Lancashire bibliography 7. Manchester: Joint Committee on the Lancashire bibliography, 1974.

TURNER, P.M. *Lancashire history: historical period, Stuart,* ed. Sidney Horrocks. A contribution towards a Lancashire Bibliography 8. Manchester: Joint Committee on the Lancashire Bibliography, 1978.

TURNER, P M. *Lancashire history: historical period, Hanover,* ed. Sidney J.Horrocks. A contribution towards a Lancashire bibliography 9. Manchester: Joint Committee on the Lancashire Bibliography, 1978.

Other volumes in this series are mentioned at the appropriate places elsewhere in this bibliograhy. For an up to date overview of historical writings on Lancashire, which deserves wide reading, see:

KERMODE, JENNY. 'Lancashire', in CURRIE, C.R.J., & LEWIS, C.P., eds. *English County Histories: a Guide.* Stroud: Alan Sutton, 1994, 216-27.

Current publications on Lancashire history are listed in:

'Bibliography', *Manchester region history review* 1- , 1987- , passim. Annual.

'Review of periodical literature and occasional publications', *Northern history* 1- , 1966- , *passim.*

'Annotated regional bibliography', *Regional bulletin [of the Centre for North-West Regional studies]* N.S., 1-, 1987-, *passim.*

Older bibliographies include:

FISHWICK, HENRY. *The Lancashire Library: a bibliographical account of books on topography, biography, history, science and miscellaneous literature relating to the County Palatire, including an account of Lancashire tracts, pamphlets and sermons printed before the year 1720, with collations, & bibliographical, critical and biographical notes on the books and authors.* George Routledge and Sons, 1875.

FOLKHARD, H.T. *Lancashire books: a list of books and pamphlets relating to the County Palatine of Lancaster preserved in the reference department of Wigan Free Public Library.* Wigan: R.Platt, 1898.

Manchester Public Library holds a nationally important collection of genealogical books, including much local material. Its published catalogue, although now rather dated, nevertheless deserves consultation:

MANCHESTER PUBLIC LIBRARIES. *Reference library subject catalogue, Section 929: genealogy,* ed. G.E. Haslam. 3 vols. Manchester: Libraries Committee, 1956-8. Pt. 1. Pedigrees and family histories. Pt. 2. Parish registers, wills. Pt. 3. Personal and place names, epitaphs, heraldry, flags.

Two authors have written so prolifically on Lancashire history that their writings have been the subject of bibliographies:

AXON, GEOFFREY R. 'A list of the writings of Ernest Axon, F.S.A., F.L.A., 1868-1947', *L.C.A.S.,* **60,** 1948, 152-6.

AXON, ERNEST. 'List of the writings of John Eglington Bailey', *L.C.A.S.* **6,** 1888, 129-50. Lists 420 works, including many on Lancashire.

A number of bibliographies of special categories of material are available. Acts of Parliament, business histories, Parliamentary papers etc., may all contain that elusive snippet of information which you need to complete your research. These are listed in the following works:

HORROCKS, SIDNEY. *Lancashire acts of Parliament, 1266-1957.* A contribution towards a Lancashire bibliography 2. Manchester: Joint Committee on the Lancashire bibliography, 1969. This supersedes:

FRANCE, REGINALD SHARPE. *Lancashire acts of Parliament, 1415-1800.* Record Publications 3. Preston: Lancashire County Council, 1950.

HODSON, PATRICIA M., ed. *The Manchester Ship Canal: a guide to historical sources.* Lancashire bibliography 11. 1985.

HORROCKS, SIDNEY. *Lancashire business histories.* A contribution towards a Lancashire bibliography 3. Manchester: Joint Committee on the Lancashire Bibliography, 1971.

TAYLOR, IAIN C. *Liverpool social history 1820-1870: an annotated guide to the use of government reports and papers.* Liverpool: Liverpool History Resources Committee, 1972.

For theses, see:

LAWLER, UNITY R.E. *North-West theses and dissertations 1950-1978: a bibliography.* Occasional paper 8. Lancaster: Centre for North-West Regional Studies, 1981.

WYKE, T.J. *A checklist of theses on the history of Lancashire.* Manchester: Manchester Polytechnic, [1979?]

For a general discussion of archival resources in the county — now rather dated — see:

PARKER, JOHN. 'Some materials for Lancashire history', *L.C.A.S.* **48,** 1932, 1-15.

New accessions to various Lancashire archival repositories were reported for a few years in:

'Archive accessions', *Northern history* **1-14,** 1966-78, *passim.*

Manchester and Lancashire Family History Society

This society holds a wide range of books and unpublished transcripts and the published catalogue of its library should be consulted. See:

MANCHESTER AND LANCASHIRE FAMILY HISTORY SOCIETY. *Library catalogue.* Manchester: the Society, 1991.

See also:

FORSYTH, JEAN M. 'Manchester & Lancashire Family History Society library', *M.G.* **27**(3), 1991, 11-12. Brief description.

MASON, MARNIE. 'Manchester and Lancashire Family History Society', *Family tree magazine* **3**(8), 1987, 19-20.

Public Record Office

A very wide range of material relating to Lancashire is held in the Public Record Office. This is listed in the now out-dated, but still important:

SELBY, WALFORD D. *Lancashire and Cheshire records preserved in the Public Record Office, London.* L.C.R.S. **7-8.** 1882-3.

Lancashire Record Office

The major record repository for the county is the Lancashire Record Office at Preston. A number of works are available to help you find your way around its collection. The basic listing for genealogists is now:

Finding folk: a handlist of basic sources for family history in the Lancashire Record Office. Preston: Lancashire Record Ofice, 1995. This provides details of parish register holdings and other sources such as wills, bishops' transcripts, marriage bonds, etc. It supersedes:

LANCASHIRE RECORD OFFICE. *Handlist of genealogical sources.* 9th ed. Preston: Lancashire County Council, 1989.

For comprehensive guides to the collections, see:

FRANCE, R. SHARPE. *Guide to the Lancashire Record Office.* 3rd ed. Preston: Lancashire County Council, 1985.
MARTIN, JANET D. *Guide to the Lancashire Record Office: a supplement 1977-1989.* Preston: Lancashire County Books, 1992.
Annual lists of accessions were initially published in:
FRANCE, R. SHARPE. 'The County Record Office during 1941-[46]', *H.S.L.C.* **93-9**, 1941-6, *passim.*
These are continued in:
LANCASHIRE RECORD OFFICE. *Report and annual lists of accessions.* 1951-. Title varies; also includes valuable essays on particular collections.
Some of the resources of the collection are described in:
Catalogue of an exhibition to illustrate the first ten years work of the Lancashire Record Office ... [Preston]: Lancashire County Council, 1950.
See also:
FRANCE, R. SHARPE. 'The County Record Office, Preston', *H.S.L.C.,* **92**, 1940, 77-84.
FRANCE, R. SHARPE. 'Local archives of Great Britain, VII; The Lancashire Record Office', *Archives* **2**(7), 1952, 45-51.
FRANCE, R. SHARPE. 'Business records in the Lancashire Record Office', *Business history,* **3**, 1960, 44-5. Summary list.
See also below, p. 48.

John Rylands Library

Another repository of county-wide — and, indeed, national significance — is the John Rylands Library of the University of Manchester. Its collections are discussed in:
CLAYTON, DOROTHY J. 'Sources for the history of North-West England in the John Rylands University Library of Manchester', *Bulletin of the John Rylands University Library of Manchester* **71**(2), 1989, 181-203. General survey.
MCNIVEN, PETER. 'Manchester University archive collections in the John Rylands University Library of Manchester', *Bulletin of the John Rylands University Library of Manchester* **71**, 1989, 205-26.
See also below, p.48.

B. *Local Collections*

Many local record offices and libraries have produced guides to their collections. These

are listed here, together with a number of bibliographies relating to particular localities.

Barrow

JONES, AIDAN. 'Cumbrian Record Office: Barrow in Furness', *Family tree magazine* **2**(6), 1986, 15-16.

Bolton

A guide to the Bolton Archive Service. Bolton: Bolton Archive Service, 1988.
Handlist of registers. 2nd ed. Bolton: Bolton Reference Library and Archives Service, 1994. Lists workhouse and school admission registers.
Tracing your ancestors at Bolton: Bolton Reference Library and Archives. Bolton: Bolton Archives and Local Studies Service, 1978. Lists resources.

Burnley

ABRAM, W.A. 'Sources of original materials for a history of Burnley', *Burnley Literary and Scientific Club transactions* **1**, 1884, 82-8. Survey of archival sources, now outdated but may still be useful.
The Lancashire Library's Burnley District: Directory of Local Studies resources. Burnley: Burnley District Library, 1992.

Bury

HIRST, RITA. *Routes: a guide to family history in the Bury area.* 3rd ed. Bury: Bury Libraries, 1992.

Chorley

SHUTTLEWORTH, DAVID. 'Local studies in Chorley', *Manchester region history review* **8**, 1994, 83-6. Description of library collection.
ELLIS, MILDRED. *The local wotwegot: a catalogue of the Colne collection of local historical material* ... Colne Library publication 4. Colne: Colne Library, 1974.

Knowsley

BURGESS, BRENDA M. *Tracing your family history in the Knowsley area at Huyton Library.* Huyton: Knowsley Local Studies and Archives Library, 1989.
SCRAGG, T.W. 'Knowsley Local Studies Collection', *L.F.H.* **3**(3), 1981, 6-9. Brief description.

Liverpool

HODSON, J.H. 'The Liverpool Record Office', *Society of Local Archivists bulletin* **13**, 1954, 39-41.

SAXTON, EVELINE B. 'The Binns family of Liverpool and the Binns collection in the Liverpool Public Library', *H.S.L.C.* **111**, 1959, 167-80. The Binns collection forms the nucleus of Liverpool Record Office.

'Liverpool City Libraries, Record Office and Local History Dept. Recent accessions January 1981-July 1982', *L.F.H.* **4**(4), 1982, 70 and *passim*.

Liverpool prints and documents: catalogue of maps, plans, views, portraits, memoirs, literature, &c., in the Reference Library relating to Liverpool and serving to illustrate its history, biography, administration, commerce and general condition and progress from early times. Liverpool: Library Museum and Arts Committee, 1908.

HAMPSON, G. 'Business records in the Liverpool Record Office', *Business history* **1**, 1958, 126-7. Brief note.

Manchester

A short bibliography of Victorian Manchester. Manchester: Victorian Society Manchester Group, 1988. Brief.

WYKE, T.J. 'Nineteenth century Manchester: a preliminary bibliography', in KIDD, ALAN J., & ROBERTS, K.W. eds. *City, class and culture: studies of social policy and cultural production in Victorian Manchester.* Manchester: Manchester University Press, 1985, 218-71.

Greater Manchester Record Office

MCKERNAN, VINCENT, & HODKINSON, JANE. *Guide to Greater Manchester County Record Office.* Manchester: [The Office], 1992.

PATCH, MAUREEN & MCKERNAN, VINCENT. 'Greater Manchester County Record Office', *Manchester region history review* **7**, 1993, 113-8.

Summary guide to collections. 2nd ed. Manchester: Greater Manchester County Record Office, 1988.

Manchester Local Studies Unit

BOND, RICHARD. 'Manchester Local Studies Unit', *M.G.* **28**(1), 1992, 4-8.

BOWER, JOAN. 'Resources in Manchester City Library', *North Cheshire family historian* **4**(1), 1977, 10-12.

'Manchester Local Studies Unit: Manchester Central Library: microfilm/microfiche self-service area', *M.G.* **28**(1), 1992, 8 page insert. Lists some of the materials held, e.g. parish registers, census newspapers, *etc.*

RAYSON, DORA. 'The papers of William Farrer (1861-1924) in the Manchester Central Library', *Archives* **10**(48), 1972, 154-7. Papers of a Manchester antiquary, including many deeds, antiquarian notes, and papers of Ecroyd, Clayton and Hodgkinson families.

The 80 volume collection of antiquarian notes assembled by John Owen is of prime importance for Manchester genealogists; it includes innumerable monumental inscriptions, parish register extracts, and other genealogical memoranda. See:

AXON, ERNEST. 'The Owen mss. (in the Free Reference Library, Manchester)', *L.C.A.S.* **17**, 1899, 48-63.

AXON, ERNEST. *Index to the Owen mss. in the Free Reference Library.* Manchester: The Library, 1900.

SIMPSON, JOYCE. 'Owens mss.', *M.G.* **19**(4) 1983, 107-8. Lists surnames mentioned.

Chetham Library

POWELL, MICHAEL. 'Chetham's Library, Manchester', *Local Historian* **20**(1), 1990, 31-6. Useful discussion.

POWELL, MICHAEL. 'Family history material in Chetham's Library', *M.G.* **27**(3), 1991, 31-2. Summary of a lecture.

POWELL, MICHAEL. 'Chetham's Library', *Manchester region history review* **2**(2), 1988/9, 25-31.

Merseyside

PROCTOR, MARGARET. *Archives on Merseyside: a guide to local repositories.* 2nd ed. Merseyside Record Office, 1992. Covers Sefton, Liverpool, Knowsley, St. Helens, and the Wirral. Brief guide.

Middleton

GARRATT, MORRIS. 'Local studies in Middleton', *Manchester region history review* **5**(2), 1991/2, 35-40. Description of local studies library collection.

Oldham

'Oldham Local Studies Library', *M.G.* **27**(1), 1991, 23-6. Brief listing of resources.

Rochdale

COLE, JOHN. *Tracing your ancestors through local libraries: a guide to genealogical sources.* Rochdale: Rochdale Metropolitan Borough Council Libraries and Arts Dept., 1983. Primarily archival guide.

FISHWICK, HENRY. *The bibliography of Rochdale as illustrated by the books in the local free public library.* Manchester: A. Ireland & Co., 1880. Bibliographic essay, reprinted from *Papers of the Manchester Literary Club* **6**, 1880.

FISHWICK, JANET. 'Miscellaneous extracts transcribed from a manuscript of the late Col. H. Fishwick', *Rochdale Literary & Scientic Society transactions* **16**, 1926-8, 31-38. Extracts from an antiquary's collection concerning Rochdale.

TODD, ANDREW. 'Notes on sources 27: Canon Raines' Lancashire manuscript', *L.* **9**(1), 1988, 40-42. Description of an antiquary's collection relating to the Rochdale area.

Rossendale

HALSTEAD, SUSAN, BOWDEN, KEN, & MARCINKIEWICZ, VICTOR. 'Local studies in the Lancashire library: collections in Rossendale District', *Manchester region history review* **2**(1), 1988, 32-6.

Tracing your ancestors in Rossendale. [ ]: Lancashire Library, 1981. Includes lists of local parish registers, directories and various other local sources.

Saint Helens

HART, ROGER. 'St. Helens Local History Library: genealogical holdings', *L.F.H.* **4**(2), 1982, 26-8. List.

Salford

PERCY, JOHN, & BLUNDEN-ELLIS, JOHN. 'University of Salford library and archives', *Manchester region history review* **6**, 1992, 85-9. Includes discussion of local history source materials.

'Salford local history library', *M.G.* **22**(4), 1986, 118-9. Brief notes on resources.

Sefton

HULL, ROGER C. *Tracing your ancestors: a genealogical guide to Sefton Libraries.* Sefton: Sefton Libraries, [198-?]

HULL, ROGER C. 'Local history resources in Sefton M.B.C.', *L.F.H.* **4**(1), 1982, 6-7. Brief note.

Tameside

Tameside includes Ashton under Lyne, Denton, Droylsden, Dukinfield, Hyde, Longdendale, Mossley and Stalybridge, as well as a number of parishes formerly in Cheshire.

Tameside bibliography. Rev. ed. Stalybridge: Tameside Leisure Services, Libraries & Heritage Division, 1992.

Guide to Tameside Archive Service. Stalybridge: Tameside Metropolitan Borough Council, 1994.

LOCK, ALICE. 'Tameside Local Studies Library', *Manchester region history review* **1**(1) 1987, 34-38.

Wigan

FOLKARD, H.T. *Wigan bibliography: a local catalogue of Wigan printed books and pamphlets and the works of authors connected with Wigan and the district, collected and preserved in the Reference Department of the Wigan Free Public Library.* Wigan: R.Platt, 1886.

A guide to genealogical sources. Wigan: Wigan Metropolitan Borough Council, [1982?]

4. PERIODICALS AND NEWSPAPERS

The Lancashire genealogist may well be confused at the wide range of historical and genealogical journals that are available. No less than five genealogical societies publish their own; these are important for contacting others who may be researching the same lines as yourself, as well as for the articles and information they contain; many articles from them are cited separately elsewhere in this bibliography. Family history society journals include:

Lancashire. [ ]: Rossendale Society for Genealogy and Heraldry, 1975- . The society was renamed The Lancashire Family History and Heraldry Society from 1985.

Liverpool Family History Society [journal]. 1976-80. Continued by: *The Liverpool family historian: the quarterly journal of the Liverpool and District Family History Society.* 1981- . The society changed its name to 'Liverpool & S.W.Lancashire Family History Society' in 1990.

The Manchester genealogist. Manchester: Manchester & Lancashire F.H.S., 1964- .

The Ormskirk & District family historian. Ormskirk: Ormskirk & District F.H.S., 1991- .

Wigan's ancient oak: annual magazine of the Wigan Family History Society. 1989- .

Historical Journals

There are two major county-wide historical journals, both of which have full indexes:

Historic Society of Lancashire and Cheshire proceedings and papers. 1848/9- . Subsequently (from 1855) *Transactions of the Historic Society of Lancashire and Cheshire.* Indexed in:

BEAZLEY, F.C. *Index of vols. I to LI, 1849-1900, of the Transactions of the Historic Society of Lancashire and Cheshire.* Supplement to *H.S.L.C.* **54.** N.S., **18.** 1904.

'Index to papers and communications, vols LII to and including vol. LXI', *H.S.L.C.,* **61,** N.S., **25,** 1909, 229-30.

'Index to volumes LXII (1910) to LXXI (1919)', *H.S.L.C.* **74;** N.S., **38,** 1922, 198-209.

'Index to volumes 72 (1920) to 85 (1933)', *H.S.L.C.* **86,** 1935, 119-36.

DICKENSON, R. 'General index, vols 86-97 (1935-45)', *H.S.L.C.* **99,** 1947, 119-29.

'General index, vols 98-110 (1946-58)', *H.S.L.C.* **110,** 1958, 205-9.

'General index, vols 111-120 (1946-58)', *H.S.L.C.* **120,** 1968, 161-8.

'Decennial index, vols. 121-128, and occasional vols. 1 and 2', *H.S.L.C.* **130,** 1981, 213-21.

'Decennial index: vols. 130-138 (1981-1989)', *H.S.L.C.* **139,** 1990, 219-29.

Transactions of the Lancashire and Cheshire Antiquarian Society. 1883- . Indexed in:

GARRATT, MORRIS. 'An index to the principal contents of *Transactions,* vol. 1 (1883)-vol. 80 (1979)', *L.C.A.S.* **82,** 1983, 169-282.

GARRATT, MORRIS. 'An index to the supplementary contents of *Transactions* vol. 1 (1883) – vol. 80 (1979)', *L.C.A.S.* **83,** 1982, 1985, 199-259.

There are also decennial indexes, which are not superseded by Garratt:

'General index ...', *L.C.A.S.* **10,** 1892, 280-338; **20,** 1903, 302-48; **40,** 1925, 265-327; **41,** 1926, 139-56; **51,** 1937, 227-309; **60,** 1948, 197-287; **70,** 1960, 103-89; **80,** 1979, 96-156.

A number of other county-wide historical journals are also available:

Lancashire and Cheshire antiquarian notes. 2 vols. Leigh: Chronicle Office, 1885-6.

The Lancashire and Cheshire historian. Macclesfield: [ ], 1965-7. 3 issues. Includes much genealogical information.

Lancashire local historian. Preston: Lancashire Local History Federation, 1983-.

Record Series

Two record societies are engaged in the publication of original source materials from North-West England – the Chetham Society and the Lancashire and Cheshire Record Society. Both have published many works of importance to genealogists, which are listed at appropriate points in this bibliography. Various lists of their publications are available in some of the works listed in Raymond's *English genealogy: a bibliography.* For a full listing of the Chetham Society's publications, see:

CROSBY, ALAN G. *A Society with no equal: the Chetham Society, 1843-1993.* C.S., 3rd series **37**. 1993.
See also:
General index to the Remains, historical and literary, published by the Chetham Society. vols. I-XXX. [ ]: Chetham Society, 1863.
General index to the remains, historical and literary, published by the Chetham Society, vols XXXI-CXIV. Chetham Society, 1893.
For the Lancashire and Cheshire Record Society, see:
HARRIS, BRIAN E. *History of the Society & guide to publications, volumes I-CXVII, 1878-1977.* L.R.C.S., **188**. 1978. Separately paginated.

Local Historical Journals
In addition to those journals which cover the whole county, there are also numerous local historical periodicals, many of the 'notes and queries' type. These are listed here.

Bolton
BARTON, B.T. ed. *Historical gleanings of Bolton & district.* Bolton: Daily Chronicle Office, 1881. 2nd series. 1882. 3rd series 1883. A 'pot pourri' of notes and gleanings.

Burnley
Retrospect: the journal of Burnley & District Historical Society. 1980- .

Bury
The Bury and Rossendale historical review and notes and queries. 2 vols. Bury: Bury Visitor, 1909-11.

Eccles
Eccles and District History Society lectures. 1968/9- .

Furness
Cumberland and Westmorland Antiquarian and Archaeological Society transactions. 1866-1900. N.S., 1901- . This is the major historical journal for Cumberland and Westmorland, but also includes many articles on Furness. A number of indexes to it are listed in Raymond's *Cumberland and Westmorland: a genealogical bibliography.*

Leyland
Leyland Historical Society bulletin. 1970-71. Continued by *Lailand chronicle: the journal of the Leyland Historical Society.* 1972- .

Longridge
Longridge and District Local History Society [transactions]. [1974(?)]- . Little for the genealogist.

Manchester
Manchester region history review. 1987- . This is indexed in:
'Manchester region history review contents, 1987-1991', *Manchester region history review* **5**(2), 1992, 59-64.
Local notes and queries from the Manchester Guardian. 132 pts. Manchester: Guardian, 1874-6.

Oldham
Local notes and gleanings: Oldham and neighbourhood in bygone times. 3 vols. Oldham: Oldham Express, 1887-9.

Over Wyre
The Over-Wyre historical journal: a journal of archaeology and local history in the Over-Wyre area of North West Lancashire. Pilling: Pilling and District Historical Society, 1981- .

Rochdale
Transactions of the Rochdale Literary & Scientific Society. 23 vols. 1878-1949.

Newspapers
Newspapers contain much information of genealogical value, especially in their births, marriages, and deaths columns. The wide range of Lancashire newspapers available are listed in:
COWLEY, RUTH. *Newsplan: report of the Newsplan project in the northwestern region, September 1986-January 1990.* Lancashire Bibliography, 1990. This also covers Cheshire and the Isle of Man, and supersedes:
SMITH, R.E.G. *Newspapers first published before 1900 in Lancashire, Cheshire and the Isle of Man: a union list of holdings in libraries and newspaper offices within that area.* Library Association Reference Special and Information Section, 1964.

5. OCCUPATIONAL SOURCES

Many works provide biographical information on persons of particular occupation. This list complements the list in Raymond's *Occupational sources for genealogists*. Historical accounts of particular occupations which do not include genealogical information are not listed here. For clergymen, see section 11, Members of Parliament, sheriffs, justices of the peace, *etc*, section 9, and teachers and students, section 12.

Ambulance Men
COOLING, ROSE. *St. John Ambulance Brigade, Ann Street, Nelson, Lancashire (demolished 1981). Roll of honour.* **N2.** [ ]: R.S.G.H., Pendle Branch, 1981. For 1914-18.

Apprentices
BARKER, F. 'List of names of apprentices sent from St. Clement Danes Parish to John Birch, of Parish of Cartmel, 10/1/1787-28/7/1801', *C.F.H.S.N.* **24,** 1982, 7-8.

BUGDEN, ERIC. 'Bound to cotton', *Hamphire family historian* 17(4), 1991, 255-6. Lists Alverstoke, Hampshire children apprenticed to a Manchester cotton factory, 1791.

DOUGLAS, ELIZABETH. 'Workhouse apprentices', *M.G.* 25(4), 1989, 19-21. Lists children from Chelsea, Middlesex apprenticed in Pendleton, late 18th c.

EMMISON, F.G. 'Essex children deported to a Lancashire cotton mill, 1799', *Essex review* 53(211), 1941, 71-81. General discussion of records from Chelmsford relating to children apprenticed in Pendleton.

SMITH, BARBARA. 'Liverpool apprentices', *C.F.H.S.N.* **44,** 1987, 15. Mainly from Kendal, Westmorland.

'Children sold into slavery: are these your ancestors?', *M.G.,* 23(3), 1987, 174-5. Lists children from Alverstoke, Hampshire, apprenticed to Manchester masters, 1791.

'Salford apprentices', *M.G.* Winter 1973, 7-8. List of indentures, 1810-21.

Architects
KENNEY, ALISON. 'Catalogue of the archives of the Manchester Society of Architects', *Bulletin of the John Rylands University Library of Manchester* **74**(2), 1992, 37-63. The archives include lists of members.

Artists
BAKER, THOMAS. 'Views of Manchester and the neighbourhood, with notices of the artists', *P.N.* **3,** 1883, 53-6, 87-9, 116-8, 162-4.

Attornies
ANDERSON, B.L. 'The attorney and the early capital market in Lancashire', in HARRIS, J.R. ed. *Liverpool and Merseyside: essays in the economic and social history of the port and its hinterland.* Frank Cass & Co., 1969, 50-77. General study; includes list of the securities of John Plumbe, mid 18th c.

Authors
HANDLEY-TAYLOR, GEOFFREY. *Lancashire authors today, being a checklist of authors born in Lancashire, together with brief particulars of authors born elsewhere who are currently working or residing in the County Palatine.* County Authors Today, 1971.

SUTTON, CHARLES WILLIAM. *A list of Lancashire authors, with brief biographical notes.* Publications of the Manchester Literary Club. Manchester: Abel Heywood & Sons, 1876.

Bank Customers
MULLEY, KEVIN. 'Notes on sources 32: the archives of the Bury Savings Bank, 1822-1972: a new source for family historians', *L.* 10(4), 1989, 42-5. Records of bank customers.

Bankers
CHANDLER, GEORGE. *Four centuries of banking as illustrated by the bankers, customers and staff associated with the constituent banks of Martins Bank Limited.* 2 vols. B.T.Batsford, 1964. v.1. The Grasshopper and the Liver Bird: Liverpool and London. v.2. The northern constituent banks. Many names of bankers.

GRINDON, LEO H. *Manchester banks and bankers: historical biographical and anecdotal.* 2nd ed. Manchester: Palmer & Howe, 1877.

HUGHES, JOHN. *Liverpool banks and bankers, 1760-1837: a history of the circumstances which gave rise to the industry, and of the men who founded and developed it.* Liverpool: Henry Young & Sons, 1906.

Bell Founders

EARWAKER, J.P. 'Bell-founders in Lancashire and Cheshire in the seventeenth and eighteenth centuries', *H.S.L.C.* 42; N.S., 6, 1890, 161-80.

Bigamists

'Bigamy in Lancashire', *M.G.* 12(2), 1976, 52-3; 12(3), 1976, 71-2; 12(4), 1976, 98-9. List of bigamists, mid-19th c., from Liverpool assize records.

Book Trades

ABRAM, W.A. 'Lancashire youths apprenticed to the London Stationers, 1565-1605', *L.C.A.N.* 1, 1885, 4-5. List.

ABRAM, W.A. 'Obituaries of Lancashire printers and booksellers, A.D. 1796-1848', *L.C.A.N.* 2, 1886, 57-8.

EARWAKER, J.P. 'Notes on the early booksellers and stationers of Manchester prior to the year 1700', *L.C.A.S.* 6, 1888, 1-26.

STEWART-BROWN, R. 'Provincial booksellers and printers', *Notes and queries* 153, 1927, 453-4. See also 154, 1928, 41 & 106. Of Lancashire and Cheshire, 17-19th c.

See also Printers

Brewers

GALL, A. *Manchester brewers of times gone by.* Swinton: Neil Richardson, 1982. Includes notes on brewers.

SIMPSON, ERIC D. 'The history of Hartley's of Ulverston', *Brewery history: the journal of the Brewery History Society* 67, 1992, 4-11; 68, 1992, 4-10; 69, 1993, 4-8. Identifies various owners, and gives many names.

Brickmakers

PRICE, R.N. 'The other face of respectability: violence in the Manchester brickmaking trade 1859-1870', *Past and present* 66, 1975, 110-32. Cites potentially useful Parliamentary papers.

SHEPPARD, PETER. 'Brickmen and manufacture in Preston before 1750', *Regional bulletin [of the Centre for North-West Regional Studies]* 8, 1994, 46-55. Includes list of 'brickmen'.

Brothel Keepers

See Prostitutes

Businessmen

Manchester of today: an epitome of results: businessmen and commercial interests, wealth and growth, historical, statistical, biographical. Historical Publishing, 1888.

See also Industrialists

Canal Boatmen

'1861 census enumeration of vessels at moorings in Blackburn', *L.* 1(4), 1975, 63-5.

'Vessels on Bridgewater Canal on night of 1861 census', *M.G.* 17(3), 1981, 87-7.

Charcoal Burners

LAMERT, JANET. 'Charcoal burners and woodcutters of Furness Fells, 1701-1851', *Regional bulletin [of the Centre for North West Regional Studies]* N.S., 5, 1991, 32-6.

Clerks

ANDERSON, GREGORY. *Victorian clerks.* Manchester: Manchester University Press, 1976. Scholarly, largely based on Liverpool and Manchester sources.

ANDERSON, GREGORY. 'A private welfare agency for white-collar workers between the wars: a study of the Liverpool Clerks Associationm 1918-39', *International review of social history* 31, 1986, 19-39. General study, clerks.

ANDERSON, G. L. 'Victorian and voluntary association in Liverpool and Manchester', *Northern history* 12, 1976, 202-19.

Clockmakers

BAILEY, F.A., & BARKER, T.C. 'The seventeenth-century origins of watchmaking in South-West Lancashire', in HARRIS, J.R., ed. *Liverpool and Merseyside: essays in the economic and social history of the port and its hinterland.* Frank Cass & Co., 1969, 1-15.

CHEETHAM, F.H. 'Notes on some Ormskirk watch and clock makers', *L.C.A.S* **51**, 1936, 1-10. Includes lists.

HAWKES, ARTHUR JOHN. *The clockmakers and watchmakers of Wigan, 1650-1850.* Wigan: The author, 1950.

HOBBS, J.L. 'Former clock and watch makers of North Lonsdale', *C.W.A.A.S.Tr.* N.S., **57**, 1957, 100-24. See also **64**, 1964, 391-2. List with biographical notes.

LOOMES, BRIAN. *Lancashire clocks and clockmakers.* Newton Abbot: David & Charles, 1975. Includes list, with brief biographical notes.

STOTT, CLIFFORD. 'Rochdale long-case clockmakers', *Transactions of the Rochdale Literary & Scientific Society* **16**, 1926-8, 86-93. Includes brief biographical notes.

Clothiers

WILLAN, T.S. 'Manchester clothiers in the early seventeenth century', *Textile history* **10**, 1979, 175-83. General study.

Club Members

WATSON, HENRY. *A chronicle of the Manchester Gentlemens Glee Club from its foundation in 1830 to the session 1905/6.* Manchester: Charles H Baker, 1906. Many names of club members.

Coalminers and Owners *etc*

CHALLINOR, RAYMOND. *The Lancashire and Cheshire miners.* Newcastle upon Tyne: Frank Graham, 1972. General study; detailed bibliography.

CROFTON, HENRY THOMAS. 'Lancashire and Cheshire coal-mining records', *L.C.A.S.* **7**, 1889, 26-73.

HOLGATE, BETH. 'The Moorfield Colliery disaster, 1883', *L.* 4(1), 1983, 11-14; 4(2), 1983, 15-16. Includes list of miners killed, from memorial at Altham, with an account of the disaster.

HOWARTH, KEN. *Dark days: memoirs and reminiscences of the Lancashire and Cheshire coal mining industry.* The author, 1978.

ORMEROD, IAN. 'The 1873 coal strike in Burnley, & the Devon and Cornwall families who came to the area', *L.* 3(3), 1980, 1719; 3(4), 1980, 17-20; 3(5), 1981, 16-19; 3(6), 1981, 11-14. Includes list of miners.

'In loving remembrance of the following unfortunate men & boys who lost their lives by the terrible explosion at Clifton Hill, Pendlebury, June 18th 1885', *M.G.* 19(1), 1983, 9. List, with ages.

The Manchester coal exchange directory. Manchester: The Exchange, 1909-64. Earlier issues list many mine-owners, colliery representatives, coal merchants, *etc.*

Convicts

WORSH, P.H. 'Notes on sources 17: calendars of prisoners at the L.R.O. (ref QJC)', *L.* 6(3), 1985, 23-4. Includes list for 1805.

BAINES, ERIC. '1851 census of Lancaster Castle: H.M.Gaol', *L.* 6(3), 1985, 10-16. Transcript.

Lancashire 1851 census: Lancaster Castle, H.M. Gaol. **L3**. 1 fiche. [ ]: [R.S.G.H.L.,] [198-?]

'Prisoners discharged from Victorian penal establishments in 1884, whose birthplace was given as Liverpool', *L.F.H.* 13(1), 1991, 9. List.

WALCOT, MICHAEL. 'The prodigal's return', *L.* 1(1), 1975, 13-14. Lancashire convicts in Portsmouth, 1851 census.

Coopers

GRANT, ALEX. 'The cooper in Liverpool', *Industrial archaeology review* **1**, 1976, 28-36. Brief note.

Cotton Masters and Merchants *etc.*

HOWE, ANTHONY. *The cotton masters 1830-1860.* Oxford: Clarendon Press, 1984. General srudy, with useful bibliography.

LONGWORTH, JAMES H. *The cotton mills of Bolton 1780-1985: a historical directory.* Bolton: Bolton Museum and Art Gallery, 1987. Includes names of some millers.

WILLIAMS, D.M. 'Liverpool merchants and the cotton trade 1820-1850', in HARRIS, J.R., ed. *Liverpool and Merseyside: essays in the economic and social history of the port and its hinterland.* Frank Cass & Co., 1969, 182-211. Includes lists of cotton importers.

The cotton spinners and manufacturers directory for Lancashire and the adjoining manufacturing districts. Oldham: J. Worral, 1891-1905. 13 issues.

'Lancashire cotton trade', *M.G.* 29(3), 1993, 20-25. Lists signatories to a 1910 petition of cotton manufacturers in favour of free trade.

Criminals
See Convicts and Policemen

Cricketers
LEDBROOKE, A.W. *Lancashire County cricket: the official history of the Lancashire County & Manchester Cricket Club, 1864-1953.* Phoenix House, 1954. Many names.

WYNNE-THOMAS, PETER. *The history of Lancashire County Cricket Club.* Christopher Holm, 1989. Includes brief biographical details of Lancashire players.

Customs Officers
JARVIS, RUPERT C., ed. *Customs letter-books of the Port of Liverpool 1711-1813.* C.S., 3rd series 6. 1954. Many names of customs officers, merchants, ships' masters and owners, *etc.*

JARVIS, RUPERT C. 'Some records of the Port of Lancaster', *L.C.A.S.* 58, 1945-6, 117-58. Includes list of Customs officers, 1773, *etc.*

WARDE, ARTHUR C. 'Liverpool's early customs collectors', *H.S.L.C.* 95, 1943, 42-56. Discussion, with some names.

WARDLE, ARTHUR C. 'The customs collection of the port of Liverpool', *H.S.L.C.* 99, 1947, 31-40. Includes list of collectors, 17-20th c.

Dockers
TAPLIN, E.L. *Liverpool dockers and seamen, 1870-1890.* Occasional papers in economic and social history 6. Hull: University of Hull Publications, 1974. General study.

Drapers
'A nest of Scottish drapers in Shakespeare Street, Manchester', *M.G.* 31(1), 1995, 63-4. From the 1891 census for Chorlton on Medlock.

Engineering Workers
MASON, MARGARET. 'An old city industry: the Atlas Works and the story of its founders', *M.G.* 21(4), 1985, 112-5. Includes many names of engineering workers, 19th c.

A register of ex-apprentices and ex-trainees of the Metropolitan Vickers Electrical Company Ltd. 4th ed. Manchester: [The Company], 1957.

Farmers
'Little Lever Farmers United Cow Club' in BARTON, B.T., ed. *Historical gleanings of Bolton and District [first series].* Bolton: Daily Chronicle Office, 1881, 97-105. Includes list of members, 1805, with biographical notes.

Firemen
BONNER, ROBERT F. 'The Greater Manchester Fire Service Museum', *Manchester region history review* 3(2), 1989/90, 39-42.

See also Insurance Agents

Footballers
SUTCLIFFE, C.E., & HARGREAVES, F. *History of the Lancashire Football Association, 1878-1928.* Blackburn: Geo. Toulmin & Sons, 1928. Includes many brief biographies.

Freeholders
EARWAKER, J.P. 'A list of the freeholders in Lancashire in the year 1600', in *Miscellanies relating to Lancashire and Cheshire* 1; L.C.R.S. 12, 1885, 225-51.

Freemasons
BEESLEY, EUSTACE B. *Freemasonry in Lancashire from the earliest times to the partition of the Province of Lancashire into two divisions in A.D. 1825-6.* Manchester: Manchester Association for Masonic Research, 1932. Many names.

RYLANDS, W.H. 'Freemasonry in Lancashire and Cheshire, (XVII century)', *H.S.L.C.* **50**; N.S., **14**, 1898, 131-202; **51**; N.S., **15**, 1899, 85-154.
'Ormskirk freemasons', *O.D.F.H.* **5**, 1993, 28-9; **6**, 1993, 1314; **7**, 1994, 7-8; **8**, 1994, 5-7. Lists of members, 1799-1802.

Glassmakers
BARKER, T.C. *The glassmakers: Pilkington: the rise of an international company, 1826-1976.* Weidenfeld and Nicolson, 1977. Includes list of staff, 1849, biographical notes on directors, folded pedigree of Pilkington, 18-20th c, *etc.* Extensive.
HARRIS, J.R. 'Origins of the St Helens glass industry', *Northern history* **3**, 1968, 105-17. Glassmakers, 17-19th c.
JACKSON, J.T. 'Long-distance migrant workers in nineteenth-century Britain: a case study of St.Helens' glassmakers', *H.S.L.C.* **131**, 1982, 113-37. General discussion.

Handloom Weavers
See Weavers

Hand-Tool Operatives
DANE, E. SURREY. *Peter Stubs and the Lancashire hand tool industry.* Altrincham: John Sherratt and Son, 1973. Includes list of hand-tool operatives.

Industrialists
CROSSLEY, R.S. *Accrington captains of industry.* Accrington: Wardleworth, 1930. Biographies of industrialists.
Fortunes made in business: series of original sketches, biographical and anecdotal, from the recent history of industry and commerce. 3 vols. Sampson Low, Marston, Searle & Rivington, 1884-7. Biographies of industrialists, mainly from Yorkshire and Lancashire.

Innkeepers
RICHARDSON, NEIL. 'Lancashire public house & licensing records 1800-1940', *L.* 3(1), 1980, 15-17.

Ashton under Lyne
MAGEE, ROBERT. *A directory of Ashton pubs and their licensees.* Manchester: Neil Richardson, 1989.

Bolton
'Loyalty of Bolton publicans in 1794', in BARTON, B.T., ed. *Historical gleanings of Bolton and District [first series].* Bolton: Daily Chronicle Office, 1881, 43-5. Includes list.

Chadderton
MAGEE, ROB. *A history of Chadderton's pubs.* Swinton: Neil Richardson, 1986.

Crompton
MAGEE, ROB. *A history of Crompton and Shaw pubs.* Manchester: Neil Richardson, 1988.

Lancaster
KENNERLEY, E. 'Lancaster inns and alehouses, 1600-1730', *Lancashire local history* **5**, 1989, 40-51. Few names.

Middleton
MAGEE, ROBERT. *Middleton pubs, 1737-1993, and their licensees.* Manchester: Neil Richardson, 1993.

Mossley
MAGEE, ROB. *Mossley pubs and their licensees, 1750-1991.* Manchester: Neil Richardson, 1991.

Oldham
MAGEE, ROB. *A directory of Oldham pubs.* Swinton: Neil Richardson, 1984.
MAGEE, ROB. *Inns and alehouses of Oldham and their licensees, 1714-1992.* Manchester: Neil Richardson, 1992.
MAGEE, ROB. *The Oldham beerhouses and their licensees, 1828-1994.* 2 vols. Manchester: Neil Richardson, 1994.

Royton
MAGEE, ROB. *A history of Royton's pubs.* Manchester: Neil Richardson, 1987.

Stalybridge
MAGEE, ROB. *Stalybridge pubs, 1750-1990, and their licensees.* Manchester: N.Richardson, 1991.

Insurance Agents
BROWN, P.C. 'Fire insurance in Liverpool', *H.S.L.C.* **78**; N.S., **42**, 1926, 3-20. Includes names of insurance agents and firemen, early 19th c.

Ironmasters

AWTY, B.G. 'Charcoal ironmasters of Cheshire and Lancashire, 1600-1785', *H.S.L.C.* **109**, 1957, 71-124. Includes pedigrees of Hall, Kent and Bridge, 17th c., also Fownes, Cotton, Booth and Bache, 16-18th c., Vernon and Kendall 18-19th c., with list of customers, 1673 and 1710/11.

FELL, ALFRED. *The early iron industry of Furness and district: an historical and descriptive account from the earliest times to the end of the 18th century, with an acount of Furness ironmasters in Scotland, 1726-1800.* Ulverston: Hume Kitchin, 1908. Many names of ironmasters.

Labourers

MARSHALL, J.D. 'The Lancashire rural labourer in the early nineteenth century', *L.C.A.S.* **71**, 1961, 90-128.

Library subscribers

'The first Liverpool library', *P.N.* **4**, 1884, 214-6. Lists subscribers, 1758.

Literary Men

Complete list of the members & officers of the Manchester Literary and Philosophical Society from its institution on February 28th 1781 to April 28th, 1896, and bibliographical lists of the manuscript volumes dealing with the officers of the Society, and of the volumes of the memoirs and proceedings published by the Society. Manchester: the Society 1896.

Marines

'Deserters from the Manchester Marine Corps, 1792-3, publicised in the *Manchester mercury* 1792', *M.G.* **17**(4), 1981, 106-7. List.

Mathematicians

WILKINSON, T.T. 'Biographical notices of some Liverpool mathematicians', *H.S.L.C.* **14**; N.S., **2**, 1862, 29-40. 18-19th c.

Medical Practitioners, *etc.*

BICKERTON, THOMAS H. *A medical history of Liverpool from the earliest days to the year 1920.* John Murray, 1936. Includes list of medical practitioners before 1749, *etc*.

BROCKBANK, EDWARD MANSFIELD. *A centenary history of the Manchester Medical Society, with biographical notes of its first president, secretaries and honorary librarian.* Manchester: Sherratt & Hughes, 1934. Includes list of office bearers.

FRANCE, R. SHARPE. 'The archives of Lancaster Asylum', *Society of Local Archivists bulletin* **12**, 1953, 36-7. List of records relating to staff and patients, mainly 19th c., and including burial registers.

MACALISTER, CHARLES J. *The origin and history of the Liverpool Royal Southern Hospital, with personal reminiscences.* Liverpool: W.B.Jones and Co., 1936. Includes 'biographical notes on members of the committee, 1842-1936.'

Annual report of the Manchester Medical Society. Manchester: the Society, 1902-8. Includes lists of members. Other years may also be available.

See also Patients

Merchants

See Customs Officers

Mill Workers

'The strike at Sir E. Armitage & Sons, Pendleton, 1850', *M.G.* **27**(1), 1991, 3-8. List of mill workers.

Miners

BURT, ROGER, et al. *The Lancashire & Westmorland mineral statistics, with the Isle of Man.* Exeter: University of Exeter Dept. of Economic History, 1983. List of mines, with names of owners and managers.

FRANCE, R. SHARPE, ed. *The Thieveley lead mines, 1629-1635. L.R.C.S.* **102**. 1951. Letters and accounts, giving many names of miners, etc.

See also Coalminers and Owners *etc.*

Music Subscribers

'The window tax: a Bolton musical celebrity', in BARTON, B.T., ed. *Historical gleanings of Bolton and Distict [Second series].* Bolton: Daily Chronicle Office, 1882, 210-46. Effectively a biographical dictionary of subscribers to the music of William Lonsdale, organist of Bolton, early 19th c. Also includes window tax assesment, 1784.

Musicians.

HANSON, W. 'Musical ancestors', *M.G.* **26**(1), 1990, 18-19. Lists musicians active in 1884.

Nail Makers

'Lancashire nail makers, 1579-1646', *Lancashire Record Office report* 1957, 7-13. Based on probate records.

Naturalists

PERCY, JOHN. 'Scientists in humble life: the artisan naturalists of South Lancashire', *Manchester region history review* **5**(1), 1991, 3-10.

Needlewomen

'Genealogical information from samplers in the collection of Salford Museum and Art Gallery', *North Cheshire family historian* **1**(5)), 1972, 7. List, 18-19th c.

Papermakers

LYDON, DENNIS, & MARSHALL, PETER. *Paper in Bolton: a papermakers' tale.* Altrincham: John Sherratt and Son, 1975.

Passenger Casualties

HUGHES, JOHN. 'Was your ancestor at Waterloo (station − not battle of)', *L.F.H.* **11**, 1989, 18-19. List of casualties, 1903, mainly Southport area, when the Liverpool to Southport express crashed at Waterloo (Lancs, not London.)

WALLS, S. 'The loss of the Rothesay Castle, 1831', *L.* **8**(2), 1987, 38-41. Lists passengers and crew saved and perished.

Patients

BEAZLEY, F.C. 'Henry Park, surgeon, and his register', *H.S.L.C.* **80**, 1928, 51-7. Discussion of a book which records his Liverpool patients, 1769-1830 (but not a transcript.) Also includes monumental inscription, 1831.

See also Medical Practitioners

Pewterers

SHELLEY, ROLAND J.A. 'Wigan and Liverpool pewterers', *H.S.L.C.* **97**, 1945, 1-26. Includes various lists, 17-18th c.

Policemen

BARTLETT, MARK. 'Lancashire Constabulary war casualties', *L.* **6**(2), 1985, 20-25. List, 1914-18 and 1939-45, with brief biographical details for those killed 1939-45.

BROADY, DUNCAN. 'The Greater Manchester Police Museum', *Manchester region history review* **1**(1), 1987, 39-42.

HEWITT, ERIC J. *A history of policing in Manchester.* Didsbury: E.J. Morten, 1979. Includes extensive list of officers and men in 1877.

MIDWINTER, E.C. *Law and order in early Victorian Lancashire.* Borthwick papers 34. York: Borthwick Institute of Historical Research, 1968. General history of the police.

PARK, ANNE. 'Notes on sources, 15: Lancashire police records', *L.* **6**(1), 1985, 26-27. Brief note on records for policemen and criminals.

WALLER, STANLEY. *Cuffs and handcuffs: the story of the Rochdale police through the years 1252-1957.* Rochdale: Watch Committee, 1957. Includes list of constables, 1607-50, 1842, and 1854, *etc.*

'Policemen's enrolment records', *M.G.* **20**(1), 1984, 31-34. Includes list of police from the 1851 Manchester census.

Politicians

'Records of the Bolton Pitt Club', in BARTON, B.T., ed. *Historical gleanings of Bolton and district [first series].* Bolton: Daily Chronicle Office, 139-58 & 234-40. See also 267-9. Includes list of members, 1810, with biographical notes.

Porcelain Makers

BONEY, KNOWLES. *Liverpool porcelain of the eighteenth century and its makers.* B.T. Batsford, 1957. Includes 'short biographical notes' on porcelain makers.

Postmen

AXON, ERNEST. 'Alexander Greene (father and son) and other Manchester postmasters', *L.C.A.S.* **29**, 1911, 154-73. Includes will of Katharine Greene, 1664.

GILMAN, FRANK. 'Preston postal services from the 1660s', *L.* **12**(2), 1991, 35-7; **12**(3), 1991, 26-7; **12**(4), 1991, 32-4; **13**(1), 1992, 18-9. Includes list of postmasters, 1666-1990.

Potters

GATTY, CHARLES T. 'The Liverpool potters', *H.S.L.C.* **33**, 1881, 123-68. Includes list of potters buried at St.Peters, 1710-37, extracts from various 18th c. directories, gazetteer of potteries naming potters, *etc.*

LANCASTER, H.BOSWELL. *Liverpool and her potters.* Liverpool: W.B. Jones & Co., 1936. Includes alphabetical listing of 18th c. potters.

LOMAX, ABRAHAM. *Royal Lancastrian pottery 1900-1938: its achievements and its makers.* Bolton: Abraham Lomax, 1957. Many names, but unfortunatly no index.

See also Porcelain Makers

Printers

ARKLE, A.H. 'Early Liverpool printers', *H.S.L.C.* **68**, N.S., **32**, 1916, 73-84. General discussion.

'Scots printers in Newton-in-Makerfield', *M.G.* **25**(1), 1989, 51-2; **25**,(2), 1989, 45-6. List, 19th c.

See also Book Trades

Prisoners

See Convicts

Privateers

WARDLE, ARTHUR C. 'The early Liverpool privateers', *H.S.L.C.* **93**, 1941, 69-97. General discussion, includes list of Liverpool owned ships, their masters and owners, 1700-1756.

Prostitutes

'Manchester underworld of 1851', *M.G.* **18**(2), 1982, 48-9. Lists prostitutes and brothel keepers in the 1851 census.

Railwaymen

JONES, AIDAN. 'Was your ancestor a Furness railwayman?' *C.F.H.S.N.* **54**, 1990, 8-9. Brief discussion of sources at Barrow Record Office.

Rioters

MARTIN, CATHERINE M. 'The Blackburn loom-breakers', *L.* **15**(2), 1994, 32-6; **15**(3), 1994, 22-7. Includes list of rioters, 1826.

PRINCE, TONY. 'The Plug Plot riots of 1842 in Preston', *L.* **13**(3), 1992, 20-26. Includes names of many trade unionist rioters.

TURNER, WILLIAM. *Riot! The story of the East Lancashire loom breakers in 1826.* Lancashire County Books, 1992. Includes biographical notes on the *dramatis personae.*

'The Lancashire riots of 1715', *M.G.* **24**(1), 1988, 27-8. Lists Manchester rioters.

Sailors

'Naval enrolment certificates for North Lonsdale 1795', *C.F.H.S.N.* **24**, 1982, 17-18. Lists recruits, with ages and places of birth.

See also Dockers and Passenger Casualties

Salt Makers

TAYLOR, ROBERT. 'The coastal salt industry of Amounderness', *L.C.A.S.* **78**, 1975, 14-21. Includes list of saltmakers, 1550-1750.

Servants

HOWELL, JAMES. 'The household staff of Towneley Hall in the nineteenth century', *Retrospect: the journal of Burnley and District Historical Society* **7**, 1987, 24-5.

Shipowners and Masters *etc*

CRAIG, ROBERT, & JARVIS, RUPERT. *Liverpool registry of merchant ships.* C.S. 3rd series **15**. 1967. Lists ships and their owners, 1786-92.

JARVIS, RUPERT C. 'Liverpool statutory registers of British merchant ships', *H.S.L.C.* **105**, 1953, 107-22. Description of a source which identifies ship owners.

SCHOFIELD, M.M. 'The statutory registers of British merchant ships for North Lancashire in 1786', *H.S.L.C.* **110**, 1958, 107-25. Discussion of a source for the names of shipowners and shipbuilders.

HAMPSON, ELIZABETH, ed. *The Graving Dock accounts, 1841-1879.* **L10.** 1 fiche. [ ]: L.F.H.H.S., 1988. Lists masters or owners of vessels entering the dry docks at Lancaster.

WOODWARD, D. 'Ships, masters and shipowners of the Wirral, 1550-1650', *Maritime history* 5(1), 1977, 3-26. Includes lists of vessels at Chester and Liverpool, 1565, with names of masters and crew.

'Shipping lists', *C.F.H.S.N.* **30**, 1984, 10-11. Lists masters of ships at Ulverston and Barrow, 1848.

See also Customs Officers and Privateers

Shipwrights

STEWART-BROWN, RONALD. *Liverpool ships in the eighteenth century, including the King's ships built there, with notes on the principal shipwrights.* Liverpool: University Press of Liverpool, 1932.

Slave Traders

BEHRENDT, STEPHEN D. 'The captains in the British slave trade from 1785 to 1807', *H.S.L.C.* **140**, 1991, 79-140. Includes lists of captains from Bristol and Liverpool.

SANDERSON, F.E. 'Liverpool and the slave trade: a guide to sources', *H.S.L.C.* **124**, 1972, 154-76. Bibliographical essay, listing both published works and manuscript sources.

Soldiers, Militiamen, *etc.*

With the exception of the present generation, most men have served in the armed forces — whether as a regular or in the militia. The literature on soldiering is vast; for Lancashire it is listed in the extensive:

WYKE, TERRY, & RUDYARD, NIGEL. *Military history in the North West.* Manchester: Bibliography of North West England, 1994.

The listing which follows is far from comprehensive; it includes only those works which contain lists of names, such as rolls of honour, or other information of direct interest to the genealogist. Regimental histories dealing with long periods are listed first; thereafter, the listing is chronological.

WILLIAMSON, R.J.T. *History of the old county regiment of Lancashire Militia, late 1st Royal Lancashire (the Duke of Lancaster's Own), now 3rd and 4th Battalions the King's Own (Royal Lancaster) Regiment, from 1689 to 1856 ... with a continuation to 1888 by J. Lawson Whalley* Simpkin Marshall & Co., 1888. Includes 51 nominal rolls and other returns.

WHALLEY, J. LAWSON. *Roll of officers of the old county regiment of Lancashire Militia, late 1st Royal Lancashire (The Duke of Lancaster's Own) now 3rd & 4th Battalions the King's Own (Royal Lancaster) Regiment, from 1642 to 1889.* Simpkin Marshall & Co., 1889.

HIGHAM, DON. *Liverpool volunteers 1759-1803: miscellaneous muster lists of volunteers and militia men.* 1 fiche. Liverpool: Liverpool and District F.H.S., 1988.

PREECE, GEOFF. 'The Museum of the Manchesters', *Manchester region history review* 2(1) 1988, 42-5. Includes brief description of the archives of the Manchester Regiment, 1758-1958.

WYLLY, H.C. *History of the Manchester Regiment (late the 63rd and 9th Foot).* 2 vols. Forster Groom & Co., 1923-5. v.1. 1758-1883. v.2. 1883-1922 (includes roll of officers 1758-1923).

SMYTHIES, R.H.RAYMOND. *Historical records of the 40th (2nd Somersetshire) Regiment, now 1st Battalion of the Prince of Wales's Volunteers (South Lancashire Regiment) from its formation in 1717 to 1893.* Devonport: A.H. Swiss, 1894. Includes various rolls of officers.

RAWSTORNE, J.G. *An account of the regiments of the Royal Lancashire Militia, 1759 to 1870 ...* Lancaster: H.Longman, 1874. Includes various lists of officers, *etc.*

MULLALY, B.R. *The South Lancashire Regiment; the Prince of Wales's volunteers.* Bristol: White Swan Press, 1952. Includes lists of colonels, and of honours and awards.

BANNATYNE, NEIL. *History of the Thirtieth Regiment, now the First Battalion, East Lancashire Regiment 1689-1881.* Liverpool: Littlebury Bros., 1923. Includes roll of officers, 1689-1881.

RAIKES, GEORGE ALFRED. *Roll of the officers of the York and Lancaster Regiment, containing a complete record of their services, including dates of commissions &c.* 2 vols. Richard Bentley & Son, 1885.

R., J. ' Cheshire and Lancashire men in service in France in 1380-1', *Cheshire sheaf* 3rd series 33, 1939, 69-82, *passim.*

DUNS SCOTUS. 'Cheshire and Lancashire men at the battle of Agincourt, 1415', *Cheshire sheaf* 3rd series 6, 1907, 12-13. List.

POWICKE, M.R. 'Lancastrian captains', in SANDQUIST, T.A., & POWICKE, M.R., eds. *Essays in medieval history, presented to Bertie Wilkinson.* Toronto: University of Toronto Press, 1969, 371-82. 15th c.

GRATTON, J.M. 'The Earl of Derby's Catholic Army', *H.S.L.C.* 137, 1988, 25-53. Includes lists of soldiers — mainly officers — in 1642-3.

NEWMAN, P.R. 'Aspects of the Civil War in Lancashire', *L.C.A.S.* 82, 1983, 113-20. Discusses the field commanders of the Royalist army; includes list.

TRUNKFIELD, R.B. 'List of the garrison at Withenshawe Hall', *M.G.* Summer 1971, 8. In the 1640s?

E[ARWAKER], J.P. 'Officers in a Lancashire Regiment, c.1680-90', *L.C.A.N.* 1, 1885, 105-6. List.

'The Manchester Volunteers of 1783', *M.G.* Winter 1973, 2. List.

WHITAKER, GLADYS. 'Colne's tragedy: the loss of the Piedmont, 1795', *L.* 10(2), 1989, 37-42. Includes list of Colne soldiers who died.

HIGHAM, D. 'Liverpool Volunteers, 1796', *L.F.H.* 4(1), 1982, 12-13. List.

'Dec. 15th 1796', *C.F.H.S.N.* 8, 1978, 8. List of men liable to serve in the militia for Dunnerdale with Seathwaite.

'Loyal Bolton Volunteers of 1802', in BARTON, B.T., ed. *Historical gleanings of Bolton and District [first series].* Bolton: Daily Chronicle Office, 1881, 216-20. List.

'Muster roll of the Bolton Light Horse Volunteers', in BARTON, B.T., ed. *Historical gleanings of Bolton and District [first series].* Bolton: Daily Chronicle Office, 1881, 17-22. Extracts only.

G., J.D. 'Breightmet Volunteer Corps' in BARTON, B.T., ed. *Historical gleanings of Bolton and District [second series]* Bolton: Daily Chronicle Office, 1882, 174-9. List, 1803.

PRIESTLEY, KAY. 'Amounderness local militia (1808-1818)', *L.* 9(4), 1988, 43-7. See also 10(3), 1989, 15-17. Amounderness Hundred. Many names.

'The Salford volunteers of 1813', *M.G.* Spring 1973, 7 & 9. List.

'The Salford Volunteers of 1813', *M.G.* Autumn 1973, 6 & 19; Winter 1973/4, 11 & 14. List.

'1841 census of Colne Barracks', *M.G.* 21(1), 1985, 42-3.

TRUNKFIELD, R.B. 'Extracts from the 1851 census: Hulme Barracks, soldiers of the 3rd Light Dragoons', *M.G.* Winter 1971/2, 9.

KELLY, DAVID. 'The first volunteer officers in Manchester in 1859', *Manchester notes and queries* 6, 1885-6, 36. Brief list.

BECKETT, J.D. 'Manchester Wellington memorial', *M.G.* 28(1), 1992, 37-9. List of veterans at its unveiling, 1856.

HAYHURST, T.H. *A history and some records of the Volunteer Movement in Bury, Heywood, Rossendale and Ramsbottom.* Bury: Thos. Crompton & Co., 1887. Includes list of the first 105 members in 1863, *etc.*

ROBINSON, GRAHAM G. 'South African war grave inscriptions', *M.G.* 21(1), 1985, 13-14. Manchester casualties of 1899-1900.

STEPHENSON, W.H. *The Territorial Army: a short history of the 1st West Lancashire Artillery Brigade.* Southport: Robt. Johnson & Co., 1956. Includes list of officers, 1908-14.

HODGSON, JOE. 'Notes on sources 5: some sources for tracing World War military ancestors in Lancashire', *L.* 3(11), 1982, 17-18. Covers 1914-18 war.

MADDOCKS, GRAHAM. *Liverpool Pals: a history of the 17th, 18th, 19th and 20th (service) Battalions The Kings (Liverpool Regiment) 1914-1919.* Leo Cooper, 1991. Includes extensive list of Liverpool pals who died on active service during the Great War.

STEDMAN, MICHAEL *Manchester Pals: 16th, 17th, 18th, 19th, 20th, 21st, 22nd & 23rd Battalions of the Manchester Regiment: a history of the two Manchester Brigades.* Leo Cooper, 1994. Includes list of fatalities 1916-18, and of awards for valour and meritorious service, 1915-19.

KEMPSTER, F., & WESTROPP, H.C.E. *Manchester City Battalions of the 90th & 91st Infantry Brigades: book of honour.* Sherrat and Hughes, 1916. For 1914-16. Extensive; includes lists by employers.

WURTZBURG, C.E. *The history of the 2/6th (Rifle) Battalion 'The King's' (Liverpool Regiment) 1914-1919.* Aldershot: Gale & Polden, 1920. Includes extensive 'nominal roll.'

The war history of the 1st/4th Battalion the Loyal North Lancashire Regiment, now the Loyal Regiment (North Lancashire) 1914-1918. Preston: Geo. Toulmin & Sons, 1921. Includes extensive casualty lists, *etc.*

The Distinguished Conduct Medal, 1914-20, citations: King's Own (Royal Lancaster Regiment). London Stamp Exchange, [198-?]

Soldiers died in the Great War 1914-19, part 9: The King's Own (Royal Lancaster Regiment). H.M.S.O., 1921. Reprinted Polstead: J.B. Hayward & Son, 1989.

Soldiers died in the Great War, 1914-19, part 13: The King's (Liverpool Regiment). H.M.S.O., 1920. Reprinted Polstead: J.B.Hayward & Son 1989.

Soldiers died in the Great War, 1914-19, part 25: The Lancashire Fusiliers. H.M.S.O., 1921. Reprinted Polstead: J.B.Hayward & Son, 1989.

Soldiers died in the Great War, 1914-19, part 35: The East Lancashire Regiment. H.M.S.O., 1921. Reprinted Polstead: J.B.Hayward & Son, 1989.

Soldiers died in the Great War, 1914-19, Part 44: The Prince of Wales's Volunteers (South Lancashire Regiment). H.M.S.O., 1921. Reprinted Polstead: J.B. Hayward & Son, 1989.

Soldiers died in the Great War, 1914-19, part 50: the Loyal North Lancashire Regiment. H.M.S.O., 1920. Reprinted Polstead: J.B. Hayward & Son, 1988.

Soldiers died in the Great War, 1914-19, Part 59: The Manchester Regiment. H.M.S.O., 1921. Polstead: J.B.Hayward & Son, 1989.

HALLAM, JOHN. *The history of the Lancashire Fusiliers 1939-45.* Stroud: Alan Sutton, 1993. Includes list of 'honours & awards.'

Stationers
See Book Trades

Stonemasons
WHITE, ANDREW. 'Stone-masons in a Georgian town', *Local historian* **21**, 1991, 60-65. Includes list of Lancaster masons, 1756.

Tanners
'The tanning industry in 16th and 17th century Lancashire', *Lancashire Record Office report* 1960, 12-19. Based on probate records.

Textile Manufacturers
FARNIE, D.A. 'John Worrall of Oldham, directory-publisher to Lancashire and to the world, 1868-1970', *Manchester region history review* **4**(1), 1990, 30-5. Includes list of directories and textile manufacturers.

Theatrical Workers
WYKE, TERRRY, RUDYARD, NIGEL. *Manchester theatres.* Bibliography of North West England, 1994.

Tradesmen
TAYLOR, BETTY. 'The black list', *North Cheshire family historian* **18**(2), 1991, 53-6. Lists Conservative tradesmen in Warrington, 1841.

Tradesmen's Tokens
In an age when currency was in short supply, many tradesmen issued their own tokens. Studies of these frequently provide useful genealogical information. For Lancashire, see:

HEYWOOD, NATHAN. 'Lancashire and Cheshire tokens of the seventeenth century', *L.C.A.S.* **5**, 1887, 64-105. Includes list of issuers.

HEYWOOD, NATHAN. 'Tradesmens' tokens of Lancashire and Cheshire issued during the seventeenth century', *Local gleanings* **1**, 1879-80, 161-3, 201-8 & 281-8. See also 436-8 & 480.

HEYWOOD, NATHAN. 'Further notes on Lancashire and Cheshire tokens', *L.C.A.S.* **30**, 1912, 65-72.

'A short list of tradesmens' tokens in connection with some of the Lancashire tokens', *Proceedings of the Manchester Numismatic Society* **1**, 1871, 171-3. From Warrington.

Tripe Dressers

HOULIHAN, MARJORY. 'Tripe: a most excellent dish', *Eccles and District History Society lectures* 1985-7, 39-48. Includes lists of tripe dressers in Eccles, 1898-1932.

Watchmakers

See Clockmakers

Weavers

BYTHELL, DUNCAN. *The handloom weavers: a study in the English cotton industry during the industrial revolution.* Cambridge: C.U.P., 1969. General study of the Lancashire industry, early 19th c. Includes list of sources.

LYONS, J.S. 'Family response to economic decline: handloom weavers in early nineteenth century Lancashire', *Research in economic history* **12**, 1989, 45-91. General study, includes bibliography.

TODD, ANDREW. 'Notes on sources, 31: researching handloom weavers from parish registers: Booth and Dakin of Prestwich and Middleton parishes', *L.* **10**(1), 1989, 36-41. 19th c., includes pedigrees.

Woodcutters

See Charcoal burners

Woodworkers

HIGENBOTTAM, S. *Our Society's history.* Manchester: Amalgamated Society of Woodworkers, 1939. Includes biographical notes on prominent members of the Society.

6. OFFICIAL LISTS OF NAMES

Government bureaucracy thrives on the compilation of lists of names. The subjects of such lists may not appreciate their consequences, e.g. taxation, but genealogists have cause to be thankful, since many of the officially compiled lists of names enable us to locate our ancestors in time and place. For Lancashire, many published transcripts and indexes of these lists are available, and are identified here.

A. *Taxation lists*

A wide variety of Lancashire tax lists have been published. The subsidy, poll taxes, the hearth tax, and the land tax are among those represented. However, only the 1332 county-wide subsidy, and the various returns for Salford Hundred, are extensive. The following list is arranged chronologically and by place.

VINCENT, JOHN A.C., ed. *Lancashire lay subsidies, being an examination of the lay subsidy rolls remaining in the Public Record Office, London, from Henry I to Charles II.* L.R.C.S., **27**. 1893. v.1. 1216-1307. No more published.

RYLANDS, J. PAUL, ed. 'The Exchequer lay subsidy roll of Robert de Shireburn and John de Radcliffe, taxers and collectors in the County of Lancaster, AD 1332', in *Miscellanies relating to Lancashire and Cheshire,* **2**. L.R.C.S., **31**. 1896. Separately paginated.

RYLANDS, J. PAUL, ed. *The Exchequer lay subsidy roll of Robert de Shireburn and John de Radcliffe, taxers and collectors in the county of Lancashire, A.D. 1332.* Wyman & Sons, 1896.

'The names of all the gentlemen of the best callinge within the countye of Lancaster wherof choyse ys to to be made of a c'ten number to lend unto her Matte moneye vpon privie seals in Janvarye 1588', *Chetham miscellanies* **3**. C.S., O.S., **57**. 1862. Separately paginated.

'Armada subscription', *M.G.* **26**(3), 1990, 55-6. List of Lancashire contributors to the defence of England against the Armada, 1588.

FISHWICK, HENRY. 'An account of £20,000 levied upon the County of Lancaster for the use of the parliamentary army, in 1643-4', *H.S.L.C.* **58**; N.S., **22**, 1906, 1-14. Gives names of constables and army officers.

Ashton under Lyne
BARLOW, ANGELA. 'The poll tax', *M.G.* 24(4), 1988, 244-7. Includes transcript of Ashton under Lyne poll tax, 1381.

Blackburn Hundred
DEARDEN, GORDON. 'King's Remembrancer, Exchequer Lay Subsidy, 1660 (P.R.O. ref E179/250/4)', *L.* 7(1), 1986, 15-16. See also 8(3), 1987, 14. Discussion of return for Blackburn Hundred.

Bolton
For the window tax assessment of 1784, see section 5 under 'Music subscribers.'

Dinckley
'An assessment of the window for the township of Dinckley, for the year of our Lord 1753 ...', *L.* 3(7), 1981, 8-9. Facsimile.

Eccles
MCALPINE, IAN. 'The Eccles and Monton hearth tax returns of 1666', *M.G.* 24(3), 1988, 173-4.

Farnworth
POLLARD, MARJORIE. 'Hearth tax return for Farnworth, near Bolton, 1673', *M.G.* 25(2), 1989, 29-30.

Leyland Hundred
R[YLANDS], J.P. 'A Lancashire subsidy, A.D. 1549', *P.N.* 2, 1882, 222. For Leyland Hundred.

Manchester
'The pole booke for Manchester, May ye 22d. 1690', *Chetham miscellanies* 3. 1862. C.S., O.S., **57**. 1862. Separately paginated. Poll tax assessment.

Prestwich
MCALPINE, IAN. 'The Prestwich hearth tax returns of 1663', *M.G.* 24(2), 1988, 96-8. Includes transcript.

Salford Hundred
TAIT, JAMES, ed. *Taxation in Salford Hundred, 1524-1802.* C.S., N.S., **83**. 1924. Subsidies, 1524, 1543, 1563 and 1600; hearth tax 1666, land tax 1780-1802.

EARWAKER, J.P., ed. 'Three Lancashire subsidy rolls, viz, for the Hundred of Salford, and the Hundred of Leyland, 1628, together with a recusant roll for the Hundred of Leyland in 1628', in *Miscellanies relating to Lancashire and Cheshire* 1. L.C.R.S., **12**, 1885, 131-89.

Urswick
HARRINGTON, D.W. 'Hair powder tax 1795-1861', *Family history* 8(43/45); N.S., **19/21**, 72-6. Includes lists of taxpayers for Urswick, Lancashire, 1795 and 1796. The only published transcript of this tax that I have seen.

West Derby Hundred
IRVINE, WM. FERGUSSON. 'Lancashire hearth taxes', *H.S.L.C.* **52**; N.S. **16**, 1900, 127-38. Includes transcript for West Derby Hundred, 1662 and 1673.

'Selection from the ancient papers of the Moore family, formerly of Liverpool and Bank Hall: subsidy in West Derby Hundred', *H.S.L.C.* **39**; N.S., **3**, 1887, 159-64. Subsidies of 1514 and 1624.

WILSON, G.J. 'The land tax and West Derby hundred, 1780-1831', *H.S.L.C.* **129**, 1980, 63-91. Discussion of its operation and use.

Widnes
Land ownership in Widnes and its environs 1776-1873. Halton historical publications 7. Halton: Halton Borough Council, 1988. Includes land tax assessments, 1781-1831, jurors' lists, 1776-1832; voters lists, 1833-66; landowners census, 1873; Cronton rate assessment. Covers Bold, Cuerdley, Ditton, Hale and Halewood.

B. *Oaths of Allegiance*
Rebellion has frequently threatened the stability of English governments. One method of countering this threat has been the demand for an oath of loyalty. At the outbreak of the Civil War in 1641/2, Parliament required every adult male to

make such an oath; the resultant Protestation returns, which still survive, contain the signatures or marks of everyone who took the oath. This is an invaluable source for genealogists. However, only a few of the Lancashire returns are in print; these are listed here. Reference should also be made to section 2 above.

Entwistle
DALTON, ADA. 'The 1642 Protestation return for Entwistle, Edgeworth and Quarlton', *M.G.* 15(3), 1979, 67-8.

Flixton
LEWIS, GRAHAM. 'The male inhabitants of Flixton parish, 1641', *M.G.* 17(1), 1981, 18. Protestation return.

Manchester
'The protestation of 1641-2 in Manchester', *P.N.* 1, 1881, 804, 102-8, 122-4, 136-40, 167-72 & 210-15. Includes brief biographical notes. See also 2, 1882, 25-6, for discussion of the 'baptismal nomenclature' as evidenced in the return.

'The Manchester protestation of 1641-1642', *M.G.* 30(1), 1994, 90-93; 30(2), 1994, 18-25.

Oldham
BUCKLEY, A.D. 'Protestation of the parish of Oldham, February 1641-2', *M.G.* 27(4), 1991, 18-22.

Over Darwen
FRANKCOM, DOROTHY [ed]. '... ? ... of Blackborne: the constables of Overderwen, James Pickup, Lawrence Hey, Marche the Sevents (1641)', *L.* 2(7), 1978, 16-17. This appears to be the protestation return for Over Darwen, although this is not stated in the transcript.

Salford
'The protestators of Salford, Kersal, Broughton and Tetlow 28 Feb., 1641-2', *P.N.* 4, 1884, 100-11 & 123-5. Protestation oath roll, with many biographical notes.

TRUNKFIELD, R.B. 'The names of such as have taken the Protestac'on within Salford ...', *M.G.* Summer 1971, 9-12; Winter 1971-2, 4-5. 1641/2.

The Restoration government also demanded an oath of allegiance from its subjects. The inhabitants of Manchester who took this oath in 1679 are listed in:
HARLAND, JOHN. 'The names of eight hundred inhabitants of Manchester who took the oath of allegiance to Charles in April 1679', *Chetham miscellanies* 3. C.S., O.S., 57. 1862. Separately paginated.

For oaths taken subsequent to the glorious Revolution see:
GANDY, WALLACE, ed. *Lancashire association oath rolls A.D. 1696.* Society of Genealogists, 1921. Reprinted 1985.

C. *The Franchise*
During the eighteenth and nineteenth centuries, Parliamentary elections were not secret, and many pollbooks listed electors and how they cast their votes. On this topic, see the works listed in Raymond's *English genealogy: a bibliography,* section 12D. Extracts from two of these pollbooks relating to Lancashire are contained in:
'Pollbook of the election of Members of Parliament for the Western Division of Cumberland', *L.F.H.S.J.* 2(1), 1978, 12. Lists voters resident in Liverpool, 1857.

CLARK, JOHN G. 'London outvoters', *Cockney ancestor* 45, 1989-90, 2-7. Lists London outvoters who voted in the Liverpool by-election of 1830.

See also:
ABRAM, W.E. 'Election of members of Parliament for Clitheroe in 1640', *L.C.A.N.* 1, 1885, 133-4. Lists burgesses and freemen who voted.

D. *The Census*
By far the most useful lists of names are the census enumerators' schedules of the nineteenth century. Many indexes and transcripts have been published; a few of these deal with a number of censuses, and are listed first; otherwise, arrangement is chronological and by place.

Bowland
Full census details 1841, 1851, 1861, 1871, 1881, with alphabetical index of surnames, maps and notes, for the township of Bowland with Leagram Lancashire. Chipping: Chipping Local History Society, [198-?]

Chipping

Full census details, 1841, 1851, 1861, 1871, 1881, with alphabetical index of surnames, maps & notes for Chipping village, Lancashire. Chipping: Chipping Local History Society, 1989.

Full census details, 1841, 1851, 1861, 1871, 1881, with surname index, maps and notes for the north part of the parish of Chipping, Lancashire, including Old Hive, Black Hall, Core, Saddle, The Grove, & Saunder Rake Bottoms. Chipping: Chipping Local History Society, 1990.

Liverpool

TAYLOR, IAIN C. 'Liverpool's institutional and quasi-institutional population in 1841 and 1851', *Local population studies* **30**, 1983, 49-53. Identifies the relevant census returns for 1851.

Maghull

SAGAR, J.H. *Combined index of 1841, 1851, 1871, 1881 censuses for the township of Maghull.* Westhead: Ormskirk & District F.H.S., [1984].

1801

Breightmet

G., J.D. 'The first census: Breightmet township', in BARTON, B.T., ed. *Historical gleanings of Bolton and District [second series].* Bolton: Daily Chronicle Office, 1882, 117-23. Return for 1801, listing 137 heads of households.
'The first census: Breightmet township', *M.G.* 23(3), 1987, 208-13. 1801 census return.

Edgworth

'The 1801 census of Edgworth', *M.G.* 11(2), 1975, 12-13.
'The 1801 census of Edgworth', *M.G.* 18(2), 1982, 40-41.

Elton

'1801 census of Elton, Bury', *M.G.* 20(4), 1984, 95-8; 21(1), 1985, 17.

Liverpool

LAXTON, P. 'Liverpool in 1801: a manuscript return for the first national census of population', *H.S.L.C.* **130**, 1981, 73-113. Includes some extracts, but not a full transcript.

Winwick

'The 1801 census for Winwick with Hulme', *North Cheshire family historian* **5**(1), 1978, 8-15. Lists 96 households.

1811

Bolton

1811 census of Great Bolton. 2 fiche. [Bolton]: B.D.F.H.S., 1982. Index to enumeration schedules for Bolton town centre.

Todmorden

JONES, BRIAN. *1811 census listing of the townships of Todmorden & Walsden in the parish of Rochdale.* Bradford: B. Jones, 1995.

1821

Bolton

1821 census of Great Bolton. 2 fiche. [Bolton]: B.D.F.H.S., 1982. Index to enumerator's schedule for Bolton town centre.

1831

Bolton

1831 census of Great Bolton. 2 fiche. [Bolton]: B.D.F.H.S., 1982. Index to enumerator's schedule for Bolton town centre.

1841

Bury

'Elton Workhouse, Bury, Lancashire, 8th June 1841', 1(1), 1975, 19. Census listing.

Halton

MACGREGOR, A.J. *A transcript of the 1841 census returns for the townships of Bold, Cronton, Cuerdley, Ditton, Hale and Rainhill (part), and the Halebank section of Halewood.* Halton historical publications **3**. Halton: Halton Borough Council, 1986.

Stretford

VICKERS, DOROTHY. 'Henshaw's Blind Asylum, Stretford, Lancs', *Family History Society of Cheshire [journal]* 15(3), 1986, 13. 1841 census.

Widnes

MACGREGOR, A.J. *The 1841 census returns for the township of Widnes: an index of surnames, a directory of addresses for Widnes in 1841*. Halton historical publications 1. Halton: Halton Borough Council, 1986.

1851

COUPE, JOHN A., ed. *1851 census surname index of Lancashire*. 59 vols to date. Manchester: M.L.F.H.S., 1984-95. Some volumes in this series are published by the L.F.H.H.S. Important

MANCHESTER AND LANCASHIRE FAMILY HISTORY SOCIETY. *Index to townships in the 1851 census surname index of Lancashire*. Manchester: M.L.F.H.S., 1991.

Cartmel

CUMBRIA FAMILY HISTORY SOCIETY. *Transcript & index for the 1851 census for Allithwaite Upper and Lower, Cartmel Fell, Staveley, Broughton East, Upper Holker.* [ ]: Cumbria Family History Society, 1991.

Halton

MACGREGOR, A.J. *A transcript of the 1851 census returns for the townships of Bold, Cronton, Cuerdley, Ditton, and Hale, and for Halebank section of Halewood, with an index of surnames*. Halton historical publications 4. Halton: Halton Borough Council, 1986.

Liverpool

PARK, PETER. *Guide to Liverpool's enumeration districts in the 1851 census*. [Liverpool]: Liverpool and District F.H.S., 1989.

Index to the 1851 census for Liverpool. 34 vols to date. [Liverpool]: Liverpool & S.W. Lancashire F.H.S., 1988-94.

ASHTON, AUDREY, ed. *1851 census: Liverpool Workhouse*. 1 fiche. Liverpool: Liverpool & District F.H.S., 1988.

PARK, P.B. *An index to Cumbrians in Liverpool, 1851*. 2 pts to date. [Walton-on-Thames]: Cumbria F.H.S., [1986.] For corrections, see *C.F.H.S.N.* **61**, 1991, 11-12.

Manchester

PARTINGTON, ERIC. *1851 census of Manchester: unfilmed section of London Road Sub-District: Public Record Office ref H.O. 107/2228*. 4 fiche. Manchester: M.L.F.H.S., 1989.

SMITH, JOHN H. 'Ten acres of Deansgate in 1851', *L.C.A.S.* **80**, 1979, 43-59. Deansgate, Manchester. Analysis of the census, few names.

Ormskirk Area

PEET, G. *Index of surnames, showing numbers and incidence of occurrence in 16 parishes, viz, Aughton, Bickerstaffe, Burscough, Downholland, Halsall, Hesketh with Becconsall, Lathom, Lydiate, Maghull, Melling, Ormskirk, Rufford, Scarisbrick, Simonswood, Skelmersdale and Tarleton, for 1851 census ref H.O. 107-2196/7*. Ormskirk: Ormskirk & District F.H.S., 1985.

SAGAR, JOHN. *1851 census ref. H.O. 107-2196 covering part of West Lancashire: surname index*. Index to census returns from parts of Western Lancashire. Westhead: Ormskirk & District F.H.S., 1983.

SAGAR, J., & PEET, G. *Index of 1851 census ref. H.O. 107-2196 for the township of Aughton*. Index to census returns from parts of Western Lancashire. Westhead: Ormskirk & District F.H.S., 1984.

SAGAR, J., & PEET, G. *Index of 1851 census ref. H.O. 107-2196 for the township of Bickerstaffe*. Index to census returns from parts of Western Lancashire. Westhead: Ormskirk & District F.H.S., 1985.

PEET, G., & JANES, R. *Index of 1851 census ref. H.O. 107-2197 for the township of Burscough*. Index to census returns from parts of Western Lancashire. Westhead: Ormskirk & District F.H.S., 1985.

SAGAR, J., & PEET, G. *Index of 1851 census ref. H.O. 107-2196 for the township of Downholland*. Index to census returns from parts of Western Lancashire. Westhead: Ormskirk & District F.H.S., 1985.

SAGAR, J., & PEET, G. *Index of 1851 census ref. H.O. 107-2196 for the township of Halsall.* Index to census returns from part of Western Lancashire. Westhead: Ormskirk & District F.H.S., 1985.

PEET, GEOFFREY. *Index of 1851 census ref. H.O. 107-2197 for the township of Hesketh-with-Becconsall.* Index to census returns from parts of Western Lancashire. Westhead: Ormskirk & District F.H.S., 1985.

PEET, GEOFFREY. *Index of 1851 census ref. H.O. 107-2197 for the township of Lathom, inclusive of the villages of Bispham, Newburgh and Westhead.* Index to census returns from parts of Western Lancashire. Westhead: Ormskirk & District F.H.S., [1984?]

SAGAR, J., & PEET, G. *Index of 1851 census ref. H.O. 107-2196 for the township of Lydiate.* Index to census returns from parts of Western Lancashire. Westhead: Ormskirk & District F.H.S., 1985.

SAGAR, J., & PEET, G. *Index of 1851 census ref. H.O. 107-2196 for the township of Melling including Melling cum Cunscough.* Index to census returns from parts of Western Lancashire. Westhead: Ormskirk & District F.H.S., 1984.

COBHAM, PHILIP. *Index of 1851 census ref. H.O. 107-2197 for the township of Ormskirk.* Index to census returns from parts of Western Lancashire. Westhead: Ormskirk & District F.H.S., 1984.

SAGAR, J., & PEET, G. *Index of 1851 census ref. H.O. 107-2197 for the township of Rufford.* Index to census returns from parts of Western Lancashire. Westhead: Ormskirk & District F.H.S., 1985.

SAGAR, J., & PEET, G. *Index of 1851 census ref. H.O. 107-2197 for the township of Scarisbrick.* Index to census returns from parts of Western Lancashire. Westhead: Ormskirk & District F.H.S., 1984.

SAGAR, JOHN H., & PEET, G. *Index of 1851 census ref. H.O. 107-2196 for the township of Simonswood.* Index to census returns from parts of Western Lancashire. Westhead: Ormskirk & District F.H.S., 1984.

PEET, GEOFFREY. *Index of 1851 census ref. H.O. 107-2197 for the township of Skelmersdale.* Index to census returns from parts of Western Lancashire. Westhead: Ormskirk & District F.H.S., 1984.

PEET, GEOFFREY. *Index of 1851 census ref. H.O. 107-2197 for the township of Tarleton.* Index to census returns from parts of Western Lancashire. Westhead: Ormskirk & District F.H.S., 1.985.

Warrington Area

H.O. 107/2202 index of surnames, 1851 census: Haycock, Newton in Makerfield, Croft with Southworth, Houghton, Middleton, Arbury, Winwick with Hulme, Burtonwood, Dallam, Great Sankey, Cuerdley, and Penketh. [Warrington]: Liverpool & District F.H.S., Warrington Group, 1985.

1851 census H.O. 107/2203: index of surnames. Warrington, Latchford, Grappenhall, Thelwall, Poulton, Fearnhead, Padgate, Woolston, Martinscroft, Rixton, Glazebrook. Warrington: Liverpool & District F.H.S., Warrington Group, 1985. Cover title.

West Derby

PARK, PETER B. *A guide to West Derby's enumeration districts in the 1851 census.* Walton on Thames: the author, 1994.

Widnes

CAPENER, J.S.A., et al. *A transcript of the 1851 census return for the township of Widnes: an index of surnames.* Halton historical publications 2. Halton: Halton Borough Council, 1986.

1881

Barrow

PITCHFORD, D.R. '1881 census: Barrow in Furness', *Cornwall F.H.S. journal* **66**, 1992, 6. Cornish extracts.

Rossendale

POWELL, LOIS. 'Cornish strays in Rossendale', *Cornwall F.H.S. journal* **48**, 1988, 27. Extracts from the 1881 census.

1891

Halsall

BAXTER, BOB. '21 in house on census night, 1891', *O.D.F.H.* **4**, 1992, 26. Census schedule for the Rectory, Halsall.

D. Landowners Census

A different type of census was taken in 1873. Everyone who owned an acre or more of land is listed in:

'Lancaster', in *Return of owners of land 1873, vol.1.* House of Commons Parliamentary papers, 1874, **LXXII**, pt. 1, 611-90.

7. DIRECTORIES, MAPS AND DIALECT

A. *Directories*

Trade directories are invaluable sources for identifying people from the late eighteenth to the early twentieth centuries; they are the equivalent of the modern phone book. Innumerable directories for Lancashire were published; for a comprehensive listing see: TUPLING, G.H. *Lancashire directories 1684-1957.* A contribution towards a Lancashire Bibliography 1. Manchester: Joint Committee on the Lancashire Bibliography, 1968.

There is no point in attempting to duplicate Tupling's listing here. However, it is worth noting that quite a number of directories have been re-printed in facsimile or on microfiche; these can easily be obtained by purchase or via inter-library loan (unlike most directories, which tend to be rare). Facsimile and microfiche editions include: (in chronological order):

BAINES, EDWARD. *History, directory and gazetteer of the County Palatine of Lancaster, with a variety of commercial and statistical information.* 2 vols. Liverpool: Wm. Wales and Co., 1824. Reprinted as *Baine's Lancashire.* Newton Abbot: David and Charles, 1968. Also published on 9 microfiche in the *English census directories project* **45 & 146.** Melbourne: Gwen Kingsley & Nick Vine-Hall, 1994.

Pigot and Co.'s national commercial directory, for 1828-9; comprising a directory and classification of the merchants, bankers, professional gentlemen, manufacturers and traders, in all the cities, towns, sea-ports and principal villages in the following counties, viz. Cumberland, Lancashire, Westmoreland . . . J. Pigot & Co., 1828-9. Reprinted Norwich: Michael Winton, 1995.

Pigot's directory, 1830: Lancashire. 5 fiche. Society of Genealogists, 1992.

KELLY, E.R., ed. *The Post Office directory of Lancashire and its vicinity.* Kelly and Co., 1864. Reprinted on 6 fiche in the *English census directories project* **3.** Melbourne: Gwen Kingsley and Nick Vine-Hall, 1991. Covers whole county.

Barrowford

'Notes on sources, 4: almanacs', *L.* 3(10), 1982, 11-12; 3(11), 1982, 8-9. Extracts from various almanacks giving many death notices, 1898-1911 — especially from Barrowford.

Bolton

The Bolton directory for 1818, containing the names, trades and residence of the principle inhabitants in the town and neighbourhood ... J. Rogerson, 1818. Facsimile reprint. Bolton: Bolton and District F.H.S., 1989.

Four Bolton directories: 1821/2, 1836, 1843, 1853. Swinton: Neil Richardson, 1982. Facsimile reprint of the Bolton portions of *Pigot and Dean's directory* 1821/2, *Pigot & Son's directory* 1836, *Slaters directory* 1843, and *Whellan and Co.'s directory* 1853.

Mackies Bolton directory, with almanack for 1849. Bolton: R.M. Holden, 1848. Facsimile reprint Swinton: Neil Richardson, 1983.

Bury

J. Leigh's directory of Bury and Rochdale, 1818. Facsimile reprint, Swinton: Neil Richardson, 1982.

Chorley

Historical and descriptive account of the parish of Chorley ... to which is added a directory and list of gentry, clergy, professional men, manufacturers and tradesmen of every description ... Chorley: C. Robinson, 1835. Facsimile reprint. Chorley: Chapter One (Publishing), 1988.

Furness

PARSON, WILLIAM, & WHITE, WILLIAM. *A history, directory and gazetteer of Cumberland and Westmoreland, with that part of the Lake District in Lancashire forming the Lordships of Furness and Cartmel.* Beckermet: Michael Moon, 1976. Originally published Leeds: W. White and Co., 1829.

Leigh

The Leigh and district directory. Wigan: Wigan Heritage Service, 1994. Originally published as *Postal directory of Bedford-Leigh, Astley, Atherton, Culcheth, Kenyon, Lowton, Pennington, and Westleigh.* 1885.

Liverpool

PICTON, J.A. 'History and curiosities of the Liverpool directory', *H.S.L.C.* 29; 3rd series 5, 1877, 9-32. General analysis, 18-19th c.

SHAW, GEORGE T. 'History of the Liverpool directories', *H.S.L.C.* 58; N.S., 22, 1907, 113-62. Reprints the *Liverpool street directory 1766,* and lists other directories.

SHAW, GEORGE T., & SHAW, ISABELLA. *Liverpool's first directory: a reprint of the names and addresses from Gore's directory for 1766, to which is added a street directory for the same year.* Liverpool: Henry Young & Sons, 1907.

The Liverpool directory for the year 1766, containing an alphabetical list of the merchants, tradesmen and principal inhabitants ... Liverpool: J. Gore, 1766. Reprinted Formby: Alt Press [1988?]

SHAW, GEORGE T., [ed.] 'Liverpool's second directory 1767', *H.S.L.C.* 78; NS., 42, 1926, 147-213. Reprint. Lists 1,622 names.

Lonsdale Hundred

MANNE & CO. *A history, topography and directory of Westmoreland and of the Hundreds of Lonsdale and Amounderness in Lancashire.* Beckermet: Michael Moon, 1978. Originally published Beverley: W.B. Johnson, 1851.

Manchester

'The oldest Manchester directories', in HARLAND, JOHN, ed. *Collections relating to Manchester and its neighbourhood at various periods.* C.S., O.S. 68, 1866, 119-66. Description of directories, 1772-1815, with some extracts.

Elizabeth Raffold's directory of Manchester and Salford, 1772. Swinton: Neil Richardson, 1981. Illustrated reprint.

Manchester and Salford directory 1788. Swinton: Neil Richardson, 1989. Facsimile reprint of *Lewis' Manchester directory.*

Bank's Manchester and Salford directory ... Manchester: G. Banks, 1800. Facsimile reprint Swinton: Neil Richardson, 1982.

Preston

General and commercial directory of Preston, Blackpool, Fleetwood, Lytham St. Anne's, Poulton-le-Fylde, Garstang, Longridge, Walton-le-Dale, Leyland, Croston, Rufford and adjacent villages and townships. Preston: P. Barrett & Co., 1889. Reprinted on 4 microfiche in *English census directories project* **60**. Melbourne: Gwen Kingsley & Nick Vine-Hall, 1982.

Ramsbottom

TODD, ANDREW A. *Trade directory reprints 1818-1888 for Ramsbottom, Edenfield, Holcombe, Tottington, Walmersley and Shuttleworth.* Ramsbottom: Allen & Todd, 1986.

Wigan

The Wigan directory, with all the parishes, townships, villages and hamlets in the Wigan Union and the village of Golborne, 1869. Blackburn: J. Worrall, 1869. Facsimile reprint Swinton: Neil Richardson, 1983.

B. Maps and Placenames

The parishes of Lancashire are frequently large, and contain many separate townships. These are mapped for genealogists in:
SMITH, J.P. *The genealogist's atlas of Lancashire.* Liverpool: Henry Young & Sons, 1930. Reference may also be made to the street map of Lancashire parishes published by the Institute of Heraldic and Genealogical Studies.

For the identification of particular places, it may be necessary to consult a dictionary of place-names. The authoritative guide is:
EKWALL, EILERT. *The place-names of Lancashire.* C.S., N.S., **81**. 1922.
See also:
HARRISON, HENRY. *The place names of the Liverpool district, or, the history and meaning of the local and river names of South-West Lancashire and of Wirral.* Elliot Stock, 1898.
MILLS, DAVID. *The place-names of Lancashire.* B.T. Batsford, 1976.
SEPHTON, JOHN. *A hand-book of Lancashire place-names.* Liverpool: Henry Young & Sons, 1913.

WYLD, HENRY CECIL, HIRST, T. OAKES. *The place-names of Lancashire: their origin & history.* Constable and Company, 1911.
Further assistance may be had by consulting published maps. For a full listing, see:
WHITTAKER, HAROLD. *A descriptive list of the printed maps of Lancashire.* C.S., N.S., **101**. 1938.
See also:
'Manchester in maps and the family historian', *M.G.* **23**(3), 1987, 167-72. Guide to Manchester Local History Library's collection.
Maps of Colne and District: a classified catalogue of the collection held for reference at Colne Library. Publication 5. Colne: Colne Library, 1977.

A number of facsimile reprints *etc.,* of historic Lancashire maps are available:
BAGLEY, J.J., & HODGKISS, A.G. *Lancashire: a history of the county palatine in early maps.* Swinton: Neil Richardson, 1985.
GILLOW, JOSEPH, ed. 'Lord Burghley's map of Lancashire, 1590', *Publications of the Catholic Record Society* **4**, 1907, 162-222. Folded map with extensive notes on gentry families, mainly Catholic.
YATES, WILLIAM. *A map of the county of Lancashire, 1786.* Introduction by J.B. Harley. Birkenhead: Historic Society of Lancashire and Cheshire, 1967. Facsimile reprint.
The village atlas: the growth of Manchester, Lancashire and North Cheshire, 1840-1912. Edmonton: Alderman Press, 1989. Facsimiles of contemporary maps.
The old series Ordnance Survey maps of England and Wales . . . 8 vols. Lympne Castle: Harry Margary, 1989-91. v. 7. North Central England. v. 8. Northern England and the Isle of Man.

C. Dialect

Dialect words frequently occur in genealogical source material, and may cause confusion. The following glossaries may provide the needed explanation:
CUNLIFFE, HENRY. *A glossary of Rochdale-with-Rossendale words & phrases.* Manchester; Heywood, 1885.

DUTTON, DAVE. *Lanky spoken here: a guide to Lancashire dialect.* Hobbs with Joseph, 1978.

MORRIS, J.P. *A glossary of the words and phrases of Furness (North Lancashire).* J. Russell Smith, 1869.

NODAL, JOHN, & MILNER, GEORGE. *A glossary of the Lancashire dialect.* Manchester: Manchester Literary Club, 1875. Reprinted Bath: Chivers, 1972.

PEACOCK, ROBERT BACKHOUSE. *A glossary of the dialect of the Hundred of Lonsdale, north and south of the sands, in the County of Lancaster ...,* ed. J.C. Atkinson. Asher and Co., for the Philological Society, 1869. Supplement 2 of the Society's *Transactions,* 1867.

8. ESTATE AND FAMILY PAPERS

A. *General*

The records of estate administration — deeds, leases, rentals, surveys, accounts, *etc.* — are a mine of information for the genealogist. Many of the records have been printed in full or in part, although much more still lies untouched in the archives. Most of the records are dispersed in numerous repositories; however, enclosure acts and awards held at Lancashire Record Office, which provide invaluable evidence for the ownership of property, are comprehensively listed in:

A handlist of Lancashire enclosure acts and awards. Record publication 1. Preston: Lancashire County Council, 1946.

Tithe surveys provide similar information to enclosure awards. For a brief discussion based partially on Lancashire evidence, see:

KAIN, ROGER, & WILMOT, SARAH. 'Tithe surveys in national and local archives', *Archives* 20, 1992, 106-17.

For fire insurance plans, see:

ROWLEY, GWYN. 'Fire insurance plans', *Manchester Region history review* 3(2), 1989/90, 31-8.

The curiously named 'final concords', or 'feet of fines', constitute a major collection of deeds held at the Public Record Office. For Lancashire, they are calendared in:

FARRER, WILLIAM, ed. *Final concords of the County of Lancaster, from the original chirographs, or feet of fines, preserved in the Public Records Office, London.* L.C.R.S. **39, 46, 50 & 60.** 1889-1910. Pt.1. 1196-1307. Pt.2. 1307-1377. Pt.3. 1377-1509. Pt.4. 1510-1558.

A bookseller's collection of miscellaneous Lancashire deeds is calendared in:

'The value of old parchment deeds in genealogical and topographical research', *Topographical quarterly* 4(2), 1936, 171-80.

The John Rylands Library of the University of Manchester holds a collection of estate records which is of national importance, but of particular value for Lancashire and north-west England. For its more general collections, see section 3B above. Estate records from Lancashire are calendared in:

TYSON, MOSES. 'Hand-list of charters, deeds, and similar documents in the possession of the John Rylands Library, II(i): documents acquired from various sources', *Bulletin of the John Rylands Library* **17**, 1933, 130-77.

TYSON, MOSES. 'Hand-list of charters, deeds and similar documents in the posession of the John Rylands Library, II(3): documents acquired from various sources', *Bulletin of the John Rylands Library* **18**, 1934, 393-454.

TAYLOR, FRANK. *Hand-list of charters, deeds and similar documents in the possession of the John Rylands Library, III: miscellaneous documents acquired by gift or purchase with an index of names of persons and places.* Manchester: Manchester University Press, 1937. A futher volume, denominated IV, was published in 1975.

Solicitors archives contain many deeds and other estate records. The archives of a Colne firm are described in:

'Documents from Messrs Pilgrim & Badgery, Colne solicitors', *Lancashire Record Office report* 1960, 20-23.

B. *Duchy of Lancaster*

The estates of the Duchy of Lancaster are extensive, both in Lancashire and throughout England. A number of works list its estate records; for its governance, see section 9. For the lands which formed the nucleus of the Duchy, see:

FARRER, WILLIAM, ed. *Some court rolls of the lordships, wapentakes and demesne manors of Thomas, Earl of Lancaster, in the County of Lancaster, for the 17th and 18th years of Edward II, A.D. 1323-4.* L.C.R.S. **41**. 1901.

ARMITAGE-SMITH, SYDNEY, ed. *John of Gaunt's register.* Camden Society 3rd series **20-21**. 1911. For 1371-5.

LODGE, ELEANOR C., SOMERVILLE, ROBERT, eds. *John of Gaunt's register (1379-83).* Camden Society 3rd series **56-7**. 1937.

For discussion of a 15th c. volume recording Duchy deeds, see:

SOMERVILLE, R. 'The coucher books of the Duchy of Lancaster', *English historical review* **51**, 1936, 598-615.

A number of works list Duchy charters:

PUBLIC RECORD OFFICE. *Duchy of Lancaster: descriptive list (with index) of royal charters.* Lists and indexes supplementary series **5**(2). New York: Kraus Reprint, 1964.

HARDY, WILLIAM, ed. *The charters of the Duchy of Lancaster.* Chancellor and Council of the Duchy of Lancaster, 1845. Little genealogical information.

PUBLIC RECORD OFFICE. *Duchy of Lancaster: descriptive list (with index) of cartae miscellaneae.* Supplementary Series **5**(3). New York: Kraus Reprint, 1963.

HARDY, WILLIAM. 'Duchy of Lancaster: calendar of royal charters, William II-Richard II', *Thirty-first annual report of the Deputy-Keeper of the Public Records,* 1870, appendix, 1-41; *Thirty-fifth ...,* 1874, appendix, 1-42; *Thirty-sixth ...,* 1875, 161-205.

For court rolls and accounts, see:

'Court rolls: Duchy of Lancaster,' in *List and index of court rolls preserved in the Public Record Office, part I.* Lists and indexes **6**. H.M.S.O., 1896, 1-129 & 370-376.

TRIMMER, R. DOUGLAS. 'Duchy of Lancaster records: inventory of court rolls, Henry I to George IV', *Forty-third annual report of the Deputy Keeper of the Public Records* 1882, appendix 1, 206-32.

'Duchy of Lancaster records: inventory of the accounts of the ministers and particular receivers, Edw. to Geo. III', *Forty-fifth annual report of the Deputy Keeper of the Public Records,* 1884, appendix 1, 1-152.

C. *Private Estates*

Many families have preserved deeds and papers relating to their estates. Publications based on these papers, or listing them, are noted here where they relate to more than one locality.

Assheton

WARDLE, L. 'Notes on sources 26: the schedules of the Assheton estate papers at the Greater Manchester County Record Office', *L.* **8**(4) 1987, 35-7. Discussion of documents relating to Bury, Middleton, Radcliffe, Prestwich, Birtle and Ainsworth areas.

Bankes

BANKES, JOYCE,& KERRIDGE, ERIC. *The early records of the Bankes family at Winstanley.* C.S. 3rd series **21**. 1973. Includes memoranda book, probate inventory of James Bankes, 1617, accounts, 1667-78 and rentals, c. 1668-77.

Blundell

The Blundell of Crosby muniments', *Lancashire Record Office report* 1957, 23-7. Medieval-19th c., mainly relating to SouthWest Lancashire.

'The Blundell of Ince Blundell muniments', *Lancashire Record Office report* 1963, 8-14. Medieval-19th c.

Byrom

Byrom deeds & wills in the possession of W.H.Thomas, B.A., 1956, with notes on omissions & duplicates. Manchester: the author, 1956. Mainly concerning Manchester.

THOMSON, W.H. *The Byroms of Manchester: a unique collection of deeds and wills ...* 3 vols. Manchester: the author, [195968?] Mainly relating to Manchester, 17-18th c., includes Byrom family pedigree.

Cavendish

'The muniments of the family of Cavendish of Holker', *Lancashire Record Office report* 1962, 29-32. Relating to Holker and North Lonsdale, 16th-19th c.

Clifton

SHAW, R. CUNLIFFE, ed. *The Clifton papers: a miscellaneous collection of papers referring to the districts of Kirkham and Lytham in Amounderness, including a XVIth century rental of Sir Richard Molyneux.* Preston: Guardian Press, 1935. Clifton family estate records, also including court rolls of Clifton, Salwick and Westby-with-Plumpton, 1699-1712, list of tenants of Kirkham, 1890-94, rentals for Lytham and Westby, 1632 and 1666, *etc.*

'The Clifton muniments', *Lancashire Record Office report* 1959, 18-24.

Coke

TAYLOR, F. *Hand-list of the Crutchley manuscripts in the John Rylands Library.* Manchester: John Rylands Library, 1951.

Reprinted from *Bulletin of the John Rylands Library* **33**, 1950-51, 138-87 & 327-72. Coke family papers relating to estates in Lancashire, Derbyshire and Suffolk, medieval-17th c.

Cookson

'The Cookson of Goosnargh papers', *Lancashire Record Office report* 1962, 17-25. 19th c.

Crosse

RADCLIFFE, R.D. *Schedule of deeds and documents, the property of Colonel Thomas Richard Crosse, preserved in the muniment room at Shaw Hill, Chorley, in the County of Lancaster.* Liverpool: T. Brakell, 1895.

'Schedule of deeds and documents, the property of Colonel Thomas Richard Crosse, preserved in the muniment room at Shaw Hill, Chorley in the county of Lancaster', *H.S.L.C.* **41**; N.S., **5**, 1889, 209-26; **42**; N.S., **6**, 1890, 275-95; **43-4**; N.S., **9**, 1893, 221-40. Abstracts of deeds, 14-16th c.

Farington

The Farington of Worden muniments', *Lancashire Record Office report* 1966, 32-8. 12-19th c.

Hoghton

LUMBY, J. H., ed. *A calendar of the deeds and papers in the possession of Sir James de Hoghton, Bart., of Hoghton Tower, Lancashire.* L.C.R.S., **88**. 1936. 12-17th c., relating to estates in mid-Lancashire. Includes summary pedigree of Hoghton, medieval-19th c.

Ireland Blackburne

'The Ireland Blackburne family muniments', *Lancashire Record Office report* 1958, 7-13.

Kirkby

SCOTT, S.H., SIR. 'A calendar of the papers and documents in the posession of Mr. James Burrow of Hill Top, Crossthwaite, near Kendal', *C.W.A.A.S.Tr.,* N.S., **20**, 1920, 177-87. Calendar of 93 documents, 17-18th c., concerning the Crosthwaite (Cumberland) and Furness districts, mainly relating to the Kirkby family.

Lacy

HARLAND, JOHN, ed. *Three Lancashire documents of the fourteenth and fifteenth centuries, comprising I. The great De Lacy inquisition, Feb. 16, 1311. II. The survey of 1320-1346. III. Custom roll and rental of the manor of Ashton-under-Lyne, November 11, 1422.* C.S., O.S., **74.** 1868.

LYONS, P.A., ed. *Two compoti of the Lancashire and Cheshire manors of Henry de Lacy, Earl of Lincoln, XXIV and XXXI Edward I.* C.S., O.S., **112.** 1884.

Preston

FRANCE, R.S. *The Holker muniments.* Penrith: Herald Printing Co., 1950. Preston, Lowther and Cavendish families estate papers, mainly relating to Lonsdale Hundred, 17-18th c.

Mather

RYLANDS, J. PAUL. 'Some deeds of the Mather family of West Leigh, Lancashire, 1609 to 1632', *New England historical and genealogical register* **49,** 1895, 29-34.

Molyneux

'The Molyneux muniments', *Lancashire Record Office report* 1955, 7-11. Medieval-19th c.

Moore

BROWNBILL, J. *A calendar of that part of the collection of deeds and papers of the Moore family, of Bankhall, Co. Lanc., now in the Liverpool Public Library.* L.R.C.S., **67.** 1913. An appendix lists a further portion of the collection held by the University of Liverpool. The collection related primarily to Liverpool, but also includes records relating to properties throughout Lancashire and Cheshire, and elsewhere, 12-17th c.

MOORE, EDWARD, SIR. *Liverpool in King Charles the Second's time,* ed. William Fergusson Irvine. Liverpool: Henry Young & Sons, 1899. Survey of Moore family property, 1668. Previously edited in:

HEYWOOD, THOMAS, ed. *The Moore rental.* C.S., O.S., **12.** 1847. Includes list of mayors, bailiffs, and Members of Parliament for Liverpool, and a note on the Stanley family.

MORTON, T.N. 'The family of Moore of Liverpool: rough list of their paper records', *H.S.L.C.* **38**; N.S., **2,** 1886, 149-58. Estate papers relating to Liverpool, Kirkdale, *etc.,* in Lancashire, and to Chester and the Wirral.

Nabb

TODD, ANDREW. 'Notes on sources 36: the leases of the Earls of Derby and the Nabb families of Walmersley', *L.* **12**(1), 1991, 29-32. 17-18th c.

Norris

HEYWOOD, THOMAS, ed. *The Norris papers.* C.S., O.S., **9.** 1846. See also C.S., O.S., **12.** 1847. 17th c. papers of the Norris family of Speke.

LUMBY, J.H., ed. *A calendar of the Norris deeds (Lancashire), 12th to 15th century, from the originals in the British Museum, the University of Liverpool, and the Liverpool Free Public Library.* L.C.R.S., **93.** 1939. Relating to Speke, Garston, Allerton, Hale, Halewood, Halebank, Woolton and many other places.

Parker

'The Parker muniments', *Lancashire Record Office report* 1962, 32-40. Medieval-19th c. estate records.

Pedder

'The Pedder of Finsthwaite muniments', *Lancashire Record Office report* 1961, 25-31.

Preston

MILLS, JAMES, & MCENERY, M.J. eds. *Calendar of the Gormanston register.* Dublin University Press, 1916. Medieval chartulary of the Preston family, originally of Preston, then of Gormanston, Co.Meath.

Prestwich

EARWAKER, J.P. 'An account of the charters, deeds, and other documents now preserved at Agecroft Hall, Co. Lancaster', *L.C.A.S.* **4,** 1886, 199-220. Relating to properties throughout Lancashire and elsewhere, and to the families of Prestwich, Langley, Dauntesey, *etc.,* 12-18th c.

Rathbone
Catalogue of the Rathbone papers in the University Library, Liverpool. 2 vols. [Liverpool]: [University Library], 1959. Lists family and business papers; includes pedigree, 18-20th c.

Rigby
'The Kenyon correspondance', *Lancashire Record Office report* 1954, 17-24. Papers of the Rigby and Kenyon families of Peel Hall, 17-18th c.

Salisbury
'Records of the Lancashire estates of the Marquis of Salisbury, held in the Liverpool Record Office, reference 920 SAL', *L.F.H.S.J.* 2(1), 1978, 15-17.

Scarisbrick
LIDDLE, JOHN. 'The Scarisbrick estates', *Lancashire Record Office reports* 1977, 41-8. 19th c.
POWELL, EDWARD, ed. 'Ancient charters preserved at Scarisbrick Hall in the County of Lancaster', *H.S.L.C.* **48**; N.S., **12**, 1896, 259-94; **49**; N.S., **13**, 1897, 185-230. Deeds, medieval-17th c., of the Scarisbrick family.
'The Scarisbrick muniments' *Lancashire Record Office report* 1960, 22-31. Description of estate muniments including some material of Roman Catholic interest.

Shireburne
REA, W.F. 'The rental and accounts of Sir Richard Shireburne, 1571-77', *H.S.L.C.* **110**, 1958, 31-57. General discussion rather than a transcript; Shireburne's properties were in North Lancashire, and Wigglesworth, Yorkshire.

Shuttleworth
PARKER, JOHN, ed. *Lancashire deeds, vol. 1: Shuttleworth deeds, part 1.* C.S., N.S., **91**. 1934. No more published. 13-17th c., relating to estates at Eccleshill, Barton, and High Whitaker. Includes will of Thomas Shuttleworth, 1593.

Slynehead
'Slynehead family of Sankey, near Warrington', *L.G.* **2**, 1877, 63-4. See also 69-70. Deed abstracts, 16th c.

Standish
EARWAKER, J.P., ed. *Charters and deeds relative to the Standish family of Standish and Duxbury, Co. Lancaster.* Manchester: Albert Sutton, 1898. Mainly relating to the Wigan area, medieval-17th c.
PORTEUS, THOMAS CRUDDAS. *Calendar of the Standish deeds, 1230-1575, preserved in the Wigan Public Library, together with abstracts made by the Rev. Thomas West in 1770 of 228 deeds not now in the collection.* Wigan: Public Libraries Committee, 1933.
HAWKES, ARTHUR JOHN. *Index to the calendar of the Standish deeds, 1230-1575 by the Rev. T.C. Porteus.* Wigan: Public Library Committee, 1937.

HORWOOD, ALFRED J. 'Documents sent by Frederick Perke, esq., of Bedford Row', in HISTORICAL MANUSCRIPTS COMMISSION. *First report ...* C.441. H.M.S.O. 1874, 92-3. Medieval deeds of the Standish family of Standish.
'The families of Standish of Standish and Duxbury, near Wigan, Co. Lancaster', *L.G.* **2**, 1877, 39-44, 45-8, 49-50, 52-4, 55-7, 58-60, 61-3, 64-6, 70-72, 74-75 & 77-8. Medieval deeds; not completed.

Towneley
RAINES, F.S., ed. 'The rent roll of Sir John Townely of Townely, Knight for Burnley, Ightenhall, etc., in the County Palatine of Lancaster, anno domin 1535-6', *Chetham miscellanies* **6**. C.S., O.S., **103**. 1898. Separately paginated. Includes will, 1539.
'The Towneley-O'Hagan muniments' *Lancashire Record Office report* 1953, 10-14. Estate records.

Twenebroke
GLAZEBROOK, MICHAEL G. 'Charters relating to the family of Twenebrokes, with notes', *Genealogist* N.S., **11**, 1895, 100-108. Includes pedigree, 14-19th c.

Wilkie
WILKIE, STUART. 'Houses owned in 1854 by John Wilkes, contractor, of Preston', *L.* **11**(3), 1990, 46-7.

D. Ecclesiastical Estates and Chartularies etc.

In the medieval period, a great deal of property was owned by ecclesiastical institutions such as churches, monasteries, dioceses, etc. For the Lancashire estates of the Diocese of Chester, see:

FISHWICK, HENRY, ed. *Lancashire and Cheshire church surveys, 1649-55.* L.C.R.S. **1.** 1879. Pt. 1. Parochial surveys of Lancashire. Pt. 2. Surveys of the lands, etc., of the Bishop and Dean and Chapter of Chester, and of the warden and fellows of the Collegiate Church of Manchester

Burscough Priory

WEBB, A.N., ed. *An edition of the cartulary of Burscough Priory.* C.S. 3rd series **18.** 1970. Includes pedigrees of Scarisbrick and Latham, medieval.

Cockersand Abbey

FARRER,WILLIAM, ed. *The chartulary of Cockersand Abbey of the Premonstratensian order.* C.S., N.S., **38-40, 43, 56-7, & 64.** 1898-1909. Includes rentals, 13th & 15th c., *etc*

RAINES, F.R., ed. 'Rentle de Cockersand, being the bursar's rent roll of the Abbey of Cockersand in the County Palatine of Lancaster for the year 1501', in *Chetham miscellany* 3. C.S., O.S., **57.** 1862. Separately paginated. Also includes abstracts of 17 deeds.

Furness Abbey

ATKINSON, J.C., ed. *The coucher book of Furness Abbey.* C.S., N.S., **9, 11, 14, & 74.** 1886-1915. Final volume ed. John Brownbill.

FLOWER, CYRIL T., ed. 'The coucher book of Furness Abbey: transcript of the lost folio 70', *Chetham miscellanies* N.S., **6.** C.S., N.S., **94.** 1935. Separately paginated. 12th c.

BECK, THOMAS ALCOCK. *Annales Furnesienses: history and antiquities of the Abbey of Furness.* Payne and Foss, 1844. Includes extensive table of contents of the chartulary, biographies of abbots, *etc.*

Knights of St. John of Jerusalem

FISHWICK, HENRY. 'The Lancashire possessions of the Knights of St. John of Jerusalem', *L.C.A.S.* **28,** 1910, 1-36. Also in *Rochdale Literary and Scientific Society transactions* **10,** 1909-10, 35-43. Includes rental, 1540 of lands in the Hundreds of Leyland, Derby, Salford and Blackburn, with deed extracts.

FRANCE, REGINALD SHARPE, 'A rental of the South Lancashire lands of St. John of Jerusalem, circa 1540', *L.C.A.S.* **58,** 1945-6, 57-70.

Penwortham Priory

HULTON, W.A., ed. *Documents relating to the Priory of Penwortham and other possessions in Lancashire of the Abbey of Evesham.* C.S., O.S., **30.** 1853. Includes descent of Fleetwood family, 14-16th c.

Syon Abbey

JOHNSTON, F.R. 'The Lancashire lands of Syon Abbey', *H.S.L.C.* **107,** 1955, 41-53. Includes list of vicars and chaplains in Syon churches', 15-16th c.

Whalley Abbey

HULTON, W.A. *The coucher book or chartulary of Whalley Abbey.* C.S., O.S. **10-11, 16, & 20.** 1847-9.

COLLINS, A.J. 'The Whalley chartulary', *British Museum quarterly* **8,** 1933-4, 94-5. Brief description.

E. Local Estate Records

There are many publications relating to estate records from particular places; these are listed here. Estate records relating to more than one or two localities are listed in sub-sections B and C.

Ashton under Lyne

HIBBERT, SAMUEL. *Illustration of the customs of a manor in the North of England during the fifteenth century.* Edinburgh: Alex Smellie, 1822. Includes custom roll and rental of Ashton under Lyne, 1422. Also printed in C.S., O.S. **74,** 1868.

Bardsea

POSTLETHWAITE, T.N. 'Some papers from Bardsea Hall muniment chest', *C.W.A.A.S.Tr.* N.S., **20**, 1920, 154-76. Primarily concerning Bardsea; general discussion.
See also Much Urswick

Blawith

BRYDSON, A.P. *Some records of two Lakeland townships (Blawith and Nibthwaite), chiefly from original documents.* Ulverston: W. Holmes, [1908?] Includes various estate documents, etc., with a rate of 1763.

Bolton

'Bolton rentals', *H.S.L.C.* **69**; N.S., **33**, 1917, 146-7. Lists tenants, 1464 and 1501.
'Bolton tithes', *M.G.* **29**(1), 1993 52-4. Index of tithe payers, 1845 and 1846.
'Selections from the ancient papers of the Moore family, formerly of Liverpool and Bank Hall: Bootle court baron', *H.S.L.C.* **39**, N.S., **3**, 1887, 167-70. 1613.

Broughton

CROFTON, HENRY T. 'Broughton topography and manor court', in *Chetham miscellanies* N.S., **2**. C.S., N.S., **63**. 1909, separately paginated. Includes various lists of tenants, 17-18th c., also list of Broughton court officers 1708-1843, and Broughton, Kersall and Tetlow wills.
MCALPINE, IAN. 'Broughton manor court records', *M.G.* **27**(4), 1991, 3-6. Facsimile and transcript of record for 1705.

Burblethwaite

JONES, G.P. 'The deeds of Burblethwaite Hall, 1561-1828', *C.W.A.A.S.Tr.* N.S., **62**, 1962, 171-97. Relating to Burblethwaite; many names of tenants.

Bury

TODD, ANDREW. 'Notes on sources, 30: the Derby muniments: the records of the manors of Bury and Pilkington as a case study', *L.* **9**(4), 1988, 32-42.

Butterworth. Coldgreave

BOULTON, KENNETH, & BOULTON, MARY. 'Piethorn Valley deeds: Coldgreave in Butterworth', *L.* **5**(4), 1984, 9-13. Lists names from the deeds of a farm, 17-18th c.

Chorley

RADCLIFFE, R.D., ed. 'The Chorley survey, being an abstract of the survey taken on the 15th February 1652 of the estate of Richard Chorley of Chorley, esquire', in *Miscellanies relating to Lancashire and Cheshire* **3**. L.C.R.S. **33**. 1896, separately paginated.

Church

See Dunkenhalgh

Clayton le Moors

See Dunkenhalgh

Clitheroe

FARRER, WILLIAM. *The court rolls of the Honor of Clitheroe, in the County of Lancaster.* 3 vols. Manchester: Emmott & Co., Edinburgh: Ballantyne Press, 1897-1913. 14-17th c., extensive.
ORMEROD, MARGARET. 'Notes on sources 35: did your sixteenth century ancestors live in the Honor of Clitheroe?', *L.* **11**(4), 1990, 16-20.

Coalyeat

KOOP, H.V. 'Coalyeat, Broughton-in-Furness, 1603-1953', *C.W.A.A.S.Tr.* N.S. **54**, 1954, 184-99. Identifies tenants of the Muncaster family at Coalyeat; includes pedigree of Muncaster, 17-20th c. and calendar of deeds.

Cockey Moor

RAINES, F.R., ed. 'Examynatyons toucheynge Cokeye More, temp Hen. VIII, in a dispute between the lords of the manors of Middleton and Radclyffe', *Chetham miscellanies.* **2**. C.S., O.S., **37**. 1856, separately paginated. Various names but unfortunately no index.

Dunkenhalgh

STOCKS, G.A., & TATE, JAMES, eds. 'Dunkenhalgh deeds, c. 1200-1600', in *Chetham miscellanies* N.S., **4**. C.S., N.S., **80**. 1921, separately paginated. Relating to the Rishton family estates in Rishton, Church, Clayton-le-Moors, and Dunkenhalgh; medieval. Includes genealogical notes on the family.

Edgworth Moor

FRANCIS, JAMES J. *Enclosures of Edgworth Moor, 1795-7.* Turton Local History Society, 1986.

Ewood

WOODCOCK, THOMAS. 'Some Ewood deeds', *Chetham miscellanies* N.S. **5.** C.S., N.S., **90.** 1931. Separately paginated. Deeds 16-19th c. Includes pedigree of Gregory, 16-18th c.

Furness

BARNES, F., & HOBBS, J.L. 'Some early Furness records', *C.W.A.A.S.Tr.* N.S. **57,** 1957, 44-71. Extracts from various manorial records *etc.,* 16-17th c.

Gisburne

WEEKS, WILLIAM SELF. *An account of the court rolls of the manor of Gisburne.* Clitheroe: Advertiser & Times, 1922.

Gollinrod

TODD, ANDREW A. 'Notes on sources 12: a catalogue of Gollinrod deeds', *L.* **5**(2), 1984, 25-31. Discussion of deeds, medieval-17th c.

Great Crosby

WILLIAMS, THOMAS. 'The halmote rolls of Great Crosby', *H.S.L.C.* **117,** 1966, 191-3. Description of rolls, 15-19th c.

Hoghton

See Walton le Dale

Hornby Castle

CHIPPINDALL, W.H. *A sixteenth-century survey and year's account of the estates of Hornby Castle, Lancashire, with an introduction on the owners of the Castle.* C.S., N.S., **102.** 1939.

Ince

See Parbold

Ince Blundell

MORTON, T.N., & GIBSON, T.E. 'Ancient charters: Ince Blundell collection', *H.S.L.C.* **32,** 1880, 179-98; **33,** 1881, 265-7; **34,** 1883, 135-44. Abstracts, medieval.

Lancaster

DOCTON, KENNETH H. 'Lancaster, 1684', *H.S.L.C.* **109,** 1957, 125-42. Lists owners or occupiers of properties, from a town plan of 1684.

Layton Hawes

FRANCE, R. SHARPE. 'Layton Hawes and Marton Mere', *Fylde Historical and Antiquarian Society [journal]* **1,** 1940, 20-46. Includes list of enclosure award, 1769.

Lees

HIGSON, CHARLES E. 'The mesne field in Lees', *L.C.A.S.* **35,** 1917, 40-49. Includes names of proprietors, *etc.,* 1806-7 and 1841.

Leyland Hundred

PORTEUS, THOMAS CRUDDAS. 'The Hundred of Leyland in Lancashire', *Chetham miscellanies* N.S., **5.** C.S., N.S., **90,** 1931, separately paginated. Lists services due from tenants, 1288, rental 1563, *etc.*

Little Crosby

TYRER, FRANK. 'The common fields of Little Crosby', *H.S.L.C.* **114,** 1962, 37-48. Includes list of tenants, 1623.

WATTS, AUGUSTINE. 'Court rolls of the manor of Little Crosby, A.D. 1628 and 1634', *H.S.L.C.* **43-4;** N.S., **7-8,** 1891-2, 103-22. Includes transcripts.

Little Urswick

See Much Urswick

Liverpool

'Norris deeds concerning Liverpool', *H.S.L.C.* **72;** N.S., **36,** 1920, 75-87. Deed abstracts, 14-16th c.

'Selections from the ancient papers of the Moore family of Liverpool and Bank Hall: sale of the Liverpool chantries', *H.S.L.C.* **40;** N.S., **4,** 1888, 177-8. Lists tenants who purchased chantry lands, 16th c.

'Selections from the ancient papers of the Moore family, formerly of Liverpool and Bank Hall: Liverpool chantries', *H.S.L.C.* **39;** N.S., **3,** 1887, 165-6. Rental of chantry lands, undated.

STEWART-BROWN, R. 'The Pool of Liverpool', *H.S.L.C.* **82**, 1932, 88-135. Includes appendix listing lessees, 17-18th c.

STEWART-BROWN, R. 'The Townfield of Liverpool, 1207-1807', *H.S.L.C.* **68**; N.S., **32**, 1916, 24-72. Includes plan of 1733 naming landowners.

Lytham
'Two centuries of manorial life in Lytham', *Lancashire Record Office report* 1965, 20-24. 16-17th c.

Manchester
EARWAKER, J.P., ed. *The court leet records of the manor of Manchester from the year 1552 to the year 1686, and from the year 1731 to the year 1846.* 12 vols. Manchester: Henry Blacklock, 1884-90. Extensive.

HARLAND, JOHN, ed. *A volume of court leet records of the manor of Manchester in the sixteenth century.* C.S., O.S., **63**. 1864.

HARLAND, JOHN, ed. *Continuation of the court leet records of the manor of Manchester A.D. 1586-1602.* C.S., O.S., **65**. 1865.

'The court leet records of the manor of Manchester', *P.N.* **1**, 1881, 187-90. Brief discussion.

CROFTON, H.T. 'Extracts relating to Deansgate, Manchester, from the Newton manor court rolls between 1530 and 1687', *L.C.A.S.* **22**, 1904, 180-85.

CROFTON, H.T. 'Tithe corn book for Manchester, etc., 1584', *L.C.A.S.* **22**, 1904, 170-79. Lists husbandmen and their crops.

EARWAKER, J.P. 'Notes on the collection of deeds preserved at the East Hall, High Legh, Cheshire, with special reference to those relating to Manchester and the neighbourhood', *L.C.A.S.* **5**, 1887, 259-71.

Marton Mere
See Layton Hawes

Much Urswick
'Land or property owners in Much Urswick, Little Urswick, Stainton and Bardsea', *C.F.H.S.N.* **10**, 1979, 13-14. List, undated, but probably 19th c.

Much Woolton
GLADSTONE, ROBERT. 'Early charters of the Knights Hospitallers relating to Much Woolton, near Liverpool', *H.S.L.C.* **54**, N.S., **18**, 1904, 173-96 & 233-5. Medieval.

SMITH, B.H. 'Court book', *C.F.H.S.N.* **51**, 1989, 18-19. Names extracted from Muchland with Tover manorial court book, 1753.

Nibthwaite
See Blawith

North Meols
CHEETHAM, F.H. 'Records of the Court Baron of North Meols, 1640 and 1643, with observations on the North Meols court leet, 1884-1926', *H.S.L.C.* **84**, 1932, 11-36. Transcript of proceedings, including pedigree showing connection of Bold, Aughton and Hesketh, 16-17th c.

Parbold
HAWKES, ARTHUR J. 'Some thirteenth and fourteenth century deeds relating to Parbold, Ince, and Sutton', *L.C.A.S.* **51**, 1936, 60-74.

Penwortham
SUTTON, CHARLES W. 'Survey of the manor of Penwortham in 1570', *Chetham miscellanies* N.S., **3**; C.S., N.S. **73** 1915, separately paginated.

Piethorn
BOULTON, KEN, & BOULTON, MARY. 'The Piethorn deeds: a progress report', *L.* **9**(1), 1988, 13-18. Primarily concerned with the Turnough and Haigh families, 17-18th c.

Pilkington
See Bury

Prescot
BAILEY, F.A. 'Coroners inquests held in the manor of Prescot, 1746-89', *H.S.L.C.* **86**, 1934, 21-39. Includes list of occupations of deceased persons, giving names.

BAILEY, F.A. 'The court leet of Prescot', *H.S.L.C.* **84**, 1932, 63-85. Includes list of records.

BAILEY, F.A., ed. *A selection from the Prescot court leet and other records, 1447-1600.* L.C.R.S. **89**. 1937.

KNOWLES, JACK, ed. *Prescot records: the court rolls, 1602-1648.* Knowsley: Knowsley Library Services, 1980.

Preston

HEWITSON, ANTHONY. *Preston court leet records: extracts and notes.* Preston: George Toulmin & Sons, 1905. 1653-1813.

'Owners of premises in Fisher Gate, Preston', *L.* 12(3), 1991, 31. List.

Prestwich

MCALPINE, IAN. 'Prestwich manor court rolls', *M.G.* 26(4) 1990, 2-6. Includes transcript, 1681.

Ramsbottom

TODD, A.A. 'The title deeds of a Ramsbottom terraced house', *L.* 8(3), 1987, 32-42. Markland family, includes pedigree, late 19th c.

Rishton

See Dunkenhalgh

Rochdale

FISHWICK, HENRY. 'Rochdale manor inquisition (survey) A.D. 1610', *Transactions of the Rochdale Literary & Scientific Society* **7**, 1900-3, 90-96.

FISHWICK, HENRY, ed. *The survey of the manor of Rochdale in the County of Lancaster, parcel of the possessions of the Rt. Worshipful Sir Robert Heath, Knt., ... made in 1626.* C.S., N.S., **71**. 1913.

Salford

FRANCE, R. SHARPE. 'Sixteenth century Salford portmoot records', *H.S.L.C.* **95**, 1943, 118-22. Transcripts of rolls for 1540, 1541, 1546 and 1547.

TAIT, JAMES. 'The court leet or portmoot records of Salford 1735-1738, with a transcript of a roll of 1559', *Chetham miscellanies* N.S., **6**. C.S., N.S., **94**. 1935. Separately paginated.

Salford Hundred

BARLOW, ANGELA. 'Salford and its Hundred in the 1540's', *M.G.* **29**(4), 1993, 8-13; **30**(2), 1994, 7-12. Discussion of the court rolls of Salford Hundred; includes list of surviving records, 1323-1867.

Stainton

See Much Urswick

Sutton

See Parbold

Torver

PARK, P.B. *My ancestors were manorial tenants.* 2nd ed. Society of Genealogists, 1994. Based on the manorial records of Torver.

See also Muchland

Toxteth Park

MCCORMICK, F. 'Land leases, district of Toxteth Park, held at Lancashire Records Office ...', *L.F.H.* **7**(1), 1985, 10-12. Lists lesees and names in leases.

Turton

An abstract of the records of the manor court of Turton, 1737-1850. Rochdale: James Clegg, [1909]. Republished on 4 fiche, Bolton: Bolton & District F.H.S., [1993].

Walton le Dale

'The muniments of Sir Cuthbert de Hoghton, Bart., J.P.', *Lancashire Record Office report* 1952, 10-11. Mainly relating to Walton-le-Dale and Hoghton.

Warrington

BEAMONT, WILLIAM, ed. *Warrington in MCCCCLXV as described in a contemporary rent roll of the Legh family ...* C.S., O.S., **17**. 1849.

BEAMONT, WILLIAM, ed. 'Homage roll of the manor of Warrington, (Co. Lancaster) 1491 to 1547', in *Miscellanies relating to Lancashire and Cheshire,* **1**. L.C.R.S. **12**. 1885, 1-41.

TEMPEST, ARTHUR CECIL, MRS. 'Schedule of deeds chiefly relating to Warrington, late the property of the Mascys of Rixton, now preserved in the muniment room at Broughton Hall in Craven', *H.S.L.C.* **40**; N.S., **4**, 1888, 156-76. Medieval-17th c.

Wavertree
LEACH, INA. 'The Wavertree enclosure act 1768', *H.S.L.C.* **83**, 1931, 43-59. Includes list of enclosure documents *etc.,* in the town chest; also accounts giving many names.

Westhoughton
'West Houghton and the Cokersand Abbey chartulary, A.D.1267', *L.C.A.N.* **2**, 1866, 174-87. Includes abstracts of 27 deeds, with pedigrees of Penulbury and Prestwych, medieval, and Blenin or Blethyn de Halghton, 13-14th c.

Wigan
BEAMONT, WILLIAM. *An account of the rolls of the Honour of Halton, part of Her Majesty the Queen's Duchy of Lancaster ...* Warrington: Percival Pearse, 1879. The Honour included Wigan, Lancashire and various Cheshire manors.
HAWKES, ARTHUR J., & PORTEUS, T.C. *Calendar of the Markland deeds and papers deposited in Wigan Public Library.* Wigan: Wigan Public Libraries Committee, 1930. Mainly relating to Wigan, 13-17th c.

Winstanley
'The sale of the manor of Winstanley in 1596', *Lancashire Record Office report* 1961, 15-18.
'Winstanley court rolls', *Lancashire and Cheshire historian* **1**, 1965, 175-6; **2**, 1966, 327-8, 497-502; **3**, 1967, 569-72. Facsimile of the roll for 1665.

F. *Manorial and Other Descents*
The descents of numerous manors and other properties have been traced; many are given in some of the antiquarian and topographical works listed in sections 1 and 2. Brief notes on descents are also given in:
BRAZENDALE, DAVID. *Lancashire's historic halls.* Preston: Carnegie Publishing, 1994. Notes many names.
CHAPMAN, MARGARET G. *Lancashire halls.* Salford: Printwise Publications, 1996. Gazetteer, including brief notes on descents.

TAYLOR, HENRY. *Old halls in Lancashire and Cheshire ...* Manchester: J.E. Cornish, 1884. Includes brief notes on descents.

Many publications relate to the descent of particular properties. These are listed here.

Alston Hall
ROBERTS, MARIAN. *The story of Alston Hall.* Longridge: Alston Hall Residential College for Adult Education, 1994. Descent, 19-20th c.

Bardsea
ANDERTON, HENRY INCE 'The manor of Bardsea', *C.W.A.A.S.Tr.* N.S. **12**, 1912, 216-61. Deals extensively with the Bardsey and Anderton families, medieval-18th c., and includes some wills.

Canon Winder Hall
HUDLESTON, C. ROY. 'Canon Winder Hall and its owners', *C.W.A.A.S.Tr.* N.S., **87**, 1987, 159-69. Descent of a Flookburgh property; includes wills of Anne Preston, 1638, Elizabeth Westby, 1652, Thomas Walton, 1683 and Elizabeth Walton, 1691.

Edge Lane Hall
HAND, CHARLES R. 'Edge Lane Hall', *H.S.L.C.* **65**; N.S., **30**, 1913, 180-89. Descent, 19th c.

Gawthorpe Hall
DEAN, RICHARD. 'Gawthorpe Hall', *Regional bulletin [of the Centre for North West Regional Studies]* **7**, 1993, 25-32. Includes notes on a descent, 17-19th c.

Haigh Hall
ANDERSON, DONALD. *Life and times at Haigh Hall.* Wigan: Smiths, 1991. Descent through Bradshaigh and Lindsay, 12-20th c.

Hale
BEAMONT, WILLIAM. *Hale and Orford: an account of two old Lancashire houses, with memorials to the respective owners to the present time.* Warrington: Guardian Steam Printing Works, 1886. Ireland and Blackburne families.

Hall i' th' Wood

IRVINE, WILLIAM FERGUSSON. 'Notes on the history of Hall i' th' Wood and its owners', *H.S.L.C.* 55-6; N.S., 19-20, 1903-4, 1-41. Descent; includes wills *etc.* of Brownlow, Norris, and Crompton, 16-18th c.

IRVINE, WM. FERGUSSON. *Notes on Hall i' the Wood and its owners.* Liverpool: Henry Young and Sons, 1905.

Halton

ROPER, WILLIAM OLIVER. 'The manor of Halton', *H.S.L.C.* 50; N.S., 14, 1898, 65-76. Medieval descent.

Hoghton Tower

MILLER, GEO. C. *Hoghton Tower: the history of the manor, the hereditary lords and the ancient manor-house of Hoghton in Lancashire.* Rev. ed. Preston: Guardian Press, 1954. Descent; includes notes on tenants, 17th c., extracts from manorial records, *etc.*

Hopwood Hall

MACDONALD, C. STUART. *A history of Hopwood Hall, including the life of Cardinal Langley, Lord Chancellor (1360-1437).* Waldegrave, 1963. Descent.

Leagram

WELD, JOHN. *A history of Leagram: the park and manor.* C.S., N.S., 72. 1913. Includes manorial descent.

Liverpool. The Tower

STEWART-BROWN, RONALD. *The Tower of Liverpool, with some notes on the Clayton family of Crooke, Fulwood, Adlington and Liverpool.* Liverpool: Ballantyne, Hanson and Co., 1910. Descent.

Makerfield

BEAMONT, WILLIAM. 'The fee of Makerfield, with an account of some of its lords, the Barons of Newton', *H.S.L.C.* 24; N.S., 12, 1872, 81-130; 25; N.S., 13, 1873, 55-112. Descent, medieval-19th c.

Lancaster. New Hall

'Lancaster jottings, V: the New Hall and its owners', *H.S.L.C.* 73; N.S., 37, 1921, 189-210. 16-17th c.

Newton

See Makerfield

Orford

See Hale

Samlesbury

CROSTON, JAMES. *A history of the ancient hall of Samlesbury in Lancashire, with an account of its earlier precursors and particularly relating to the more recent descent of the manor ...* Whittingham & Wilkins, 1871. Descent; includes numerous extracts from original sources, also pedigrees of Holand, Southworth, and Braddyll.

Smithills Hall

BILLINGTON, W.D. *Smithills Hall.* Bolton: Halliwell Local History Society, 1991. Includes much information on owners, including pedigrees.

MITCHELL, MARIE. *A short history of Smithills Hall and its families, 1335 to 1990.* Bolton: Friends of Smithills Hall, 1991. Descent.

Thatto Heath. The Scholes

BARKER, T.C., & HARRIS, S.A. 'The Scholes: a sixteenth century Lancashire house', *H.S.L.C.* 113, 1961, 43-64. See also 115, 1963, 175-6. Traces descent of a Thatto Heath house.

Tottington Hall

COUPE, GLADYS. *Tottington Hall through five centuries.* Swinton: Neil Richardson, 1989.

Trafford Park

Trafford Park, past and present and Ship Canal guide. Manchester: R.S. Chrystal, 1902. Includes brief descent of Trafford.

Tytup Hall

MELVILLE, J. 'The chronological record of Tytup Hall', *C.W.A.A.S.Tr.* N.S., 75, 1975, 258-61. Descent, 18th c.

Wardley Hall

HART-DAVIS, HENRY VAUGHAN & HOLME, STRACHAN. *History of Wardley Hall,*

Lancashire and its owners in bygone days
Manchester: Sherrat & Hughes, 1908.
Descent; includes deeds, medieval-17th c.,
inquisition post-mortem of Gilbert
Sherington, folded pedigree of Worsley,
etc.

Warrington
BEAMONT, WILLIAM. *Annals of the lords of Warrington for the first five centuries after the Conquest with historical notices of the place and neighbourhood.* C.S., O.S., **86-7**. 1872-3. Descent, medieval.
BEAMONT, WILLIAM. *Annals of the lords of Warrington and Bewsey from 1587-1833 ...* Manchester: Charles Simms and Co., 1873. Pt. 1. Warrington. Pt. 2. Bewsey.

Whickleswick
BIRD, W.H.B. 'Whickleswick: a lost township', *Ancestor* **4**, 1902, 205-24. Descent; now in Eccles.

Whittington
CHIPPINDALL, W.H. 'The ancient manors of Whittington', *H.S.L.C.* **75**, N.S., **39**, 1923, 238-58. Traces descents to 17th c., includes list of tenants, early 16th c.

Withington
'The manor of Withington in earliest times', *M.G.* N.S. **2**(1), 1965, 15-16; **2**(2), 1966, 15-19. Descent, also includes notes on families.

G. Account Books etc
A number of Lancashire publications provide transcripts of household and business accounts, *etc.,* which provide much useful information on the names of servants and tradesmen, *etc.* These are listed here.

Bealey
BEALEY, F.H. 'Extracts from a cash book of Ralph Bealey of Balderstone Hall, near Rochdale', 1808-1812', *M.G.* **18**(2), 1982, 52-4. Lists persons with whom he had dealings.

Brandwood
SMITH, W.J. 'The cost of building Lancashire loom houses and weavers' workshops: the account book of James Brandwood of

Turton, 1794-1814', *Textile history* **8**, 1977, 56-76. Includes extracts, giving names of suppliers.

Fell
PENNEY, NORMAN, ed. *The household account books of Sarah Fell of Swarthmore Hall.* Cambridge: Cambridge University Press, 1920. 17th c., includes much information on both the business affairs of the family, and on the local Quaker meeting, with many names.

Latham
WEATHERILL, LORNA, ed. *The account book of Richard Latham, 1724-1767.* Records of social and economic history N.S., **15**. Oxford: Oxford University Press, 1990.

Molyneaux
CROSBY, ALAN. 'The Croxteth Hall household accounts, 1690-1693', *Regional bulletin [of the Centre for North-West Regional Studies]* N.S. **7**, 1993, 4-9. Discussion of Molyneaux family household accounts.

Nowell
GROSART, ALEXANDER B., ed. *The Towneley Hall mss. The spending of the money of Robert Nowell, of Reade Hall, Lancashire, brother of Dean Alexander Nowell, 1568-1580.* [Manchester]: Privately published, 1877. Extensive household accounts, with innumerable names.

Shuttleworth
HARLAND, JOHN. *The house and farm accounts of the Shuttleworths of Gawthorpe Hall, in the County of Lancaster, at Smithils and Gawthorpe, from September 1582 to October 1621.* C.S., O.S., **35, 41, 43, & 46**. 1856-7. Many names. Supplemented by:
'The house and farm accounts of the Shuttleworths of Gawthorpe', *P.N.* **4**, 1884, 83-5.

Stanley
FRANCE, R. SHARPE. 'A Stanley account roll 1460', *H.S.L.C.* **113**, 1961, 203-9. Account roll of the Stanleys of Knowsley and Latham; many names.

Threlfall

JENKINSON, ANDREW. 'Extracts from the farm accounts of James Threlfall of Bell Farm, Scronkey, 1861-1865', *Over Wyre historical journal* **3**, 1984-5, 24-8. In Pilling.

Towneley

WARD, J. LANGFIELD. 'The Towneley manuscript', *Burnley Literary and Scientific Club Transactions* **2**, 1884, 98-102. Descriptions of John Towneley's account book, 1601-8.

9. RECORDS OF NATIONAL, COUNTY, AND DUCHY GOVERNMENT

A. *M.P.s and other office holders*

A number of lists of members of Parliament, justices of the peace, lords lieutenants, and other officials have been published; some of them provide biographical information. For M.P.'s, see:

BEAN, WILLIAM WARDELL. *The Parliamentary representation of the six northern counties of England: Cumberland, Durham, Lancashire, Northumberland, Westmoreland and Yorkshire, and their cities and boroughs from 1603 to 1886, with lists of members and biographical notices.* Hull: Charles Henry Barnwell, 1890.

HORNYOLD-STRICKLAND, HENRY. *Biographical sketches of the Members of Parliament of Lancashire (1290-1550).* C.S., N.S., **93**. 1935.

ROSKELL, JOHN S. *The knights of the shire for the County Palatine of Lancaster (1377-1460).* C.S., N.S., **96**. 1937.

DOBSON, WILLIAM. *History of the Parliamentary representation of Preston during the last hundred years.* 2nd ed. Preston: W. & J. Dobson, 1868.

WATSON, J. BRIERLEY. 'The Lancashire gentry and public service, 1529-1558', *L.C.A.S.* **73-4**, 1963-4, 11-59. Includes lists of J.P.'s and M.P.'s, *etc.*

For Justices of the Peace, see:

WILKINSON, D. J. 'The Commission of the Peace in Lancashire, 1603-1642', *H.S.L.C* **132**, 1983, 41-66. Includes list of 168 justices of the peace.

WILKINSON, D. J. 'Performance and motivation amongst the Justices of the Peace in early Stuart Lancashire', *H.S.L.C.* **138**, 1989, 35-65. Includes brief lists of J.P.s.

FRANCE, R. SHARPE. 'Lancashire justices of the peace in 1583', *H.S.L.C* **95**, 1943, 131-3.

FRANCE, R. SHARPE. 'The Lancashire Sessions Act, 1798', *L.C.S.H.* **96**, 1944, 1-57. Includes lists of justices of the peace, 1787-98.

Lord lieutenants and their deputies are listed in:

CARTER, D.P. 'The Lancashire militia 1660-1688', *H.S.L.C.* **132**, 1983, 155-8.

For bailiffs, see:

TUPLING, G.H. 'The royal and seignorial bailiffs of Lancashire in the thirteenth and fourteenth centuries', *Chetham miscellanies* N.S., **8**. C.S., N.S., **109**. 1945. Separately paginated.

A variety of other office holders are listed in the important:

SOMERVILLE, R. *Office-holders in the Duchy and County Palatine of Lancaster from 1603.* Phillimore, 1972. Includes biographical information, and supersedes:

WILLIAMS, W.R. *Official lists of the Duchy and County Palatine of Lancaster, from earliest times to the present day, with biographical and geographical notices compiled from the records of the Duchy and Record offices.* Brecknock: the author, 1901.

B. *Duchy of Lancaster*

The existence of the Duchy of Lancaster meant that government in the county was constituted in a different way to that in other counties. The standard guide to the history of the Duchy is:

SOMERVILLE, ROBERT. *History of the Duchy of Lancaster.* 2 vols. London: the Duchy, 1953. v. 1. 1265-1603. No more published.

A general discussion of the Duchy's archival history is given in:

SOMERVILLE, R. 'The Duchy of Lancaster records', *Transactions of the Royal Historical Society* **29**, 1947, 1-17.

For a discussion of Duchy records from the genealogists' point of view, see:

BARLOW, ANGELA. 'Now if you'd said Palantine', *M.G.* **28**(2), 1992, 4-6.

BARLOW, ANGELA. 'Notes on sources 34: the Chancery Court of the County Palatine of Lancaster', *L.* **11**(3), 1990, 19-25.

Duchy records are listed in several works:

GIUSEPPI, M.S. *List of the records of the Duchy of Lancaster.* Lists and indexes **14**. H.M.S.O., 1901. Reprinted with amendments. New York: Kraus Reprint, 1963.

PUBLIC RECORD OFFICE. *Duchy of Lancaster supplementary list of records.* Lists and indexes supplementary series 5(1). New York: Kraus Reprint, 1964.

'Palatinate of Lancaster', in *List of records of the Palatinates of Chester, Durham & Lancaster, the Honour of Peveril and the Principality of Wales preserved in the Public Record Office.* Lists and indexes **40**. H.M.S.O., 1914, 52-83. Reprinted New York: Kraus Reprint, 1963.

HARDY, WILLIAM. 'Inventory and lists of the documents transferred from the Duchy of Lancaster Office ... to the Public Record Office ... 1868', *Thirtieth annual report of the Deputy Keeper of the Public Records,* H.M.S.O., 1869, appendix, 1-43.

A number of works provide full calenders of Duchy administrative proceedings in the medieval period; these are listed here. For records of the Duchy estates, see section 7B above.

STEPHEN, H.S.J. 'Duchy of Lancaster records: calendar of privy seals of the County Palatine Richard II,' *Forty-third annual report of the Deputy Keeper of the Public Records* 1882 appendix 1, 363-70.

STEPHEN, HENRY ST. JAMES. 'Duchy of Lancaster records: calendar of patent rolls, 4 Ric. II-21 Hen.VII', *Fortieth annual report of the Deputy Keeper of the Public Records,* 1879, appendix, 521-45.

HARDY, WILLIAM. 'Duchy of Lancaster: calendar of rolls of the Chancery of the County Palatine', *Thirty-second annual report of the Deputy Keeper of the Public Records.* 1871, appendix, 331-65; *Thirty-third ...* 1872, appendix, 1-42; *Thirty-seventh ...* 1876, appendix 1, 172-9.

PARKER, JOHN, ed. *Plea rolls of the County Palatine of Lancaster. Roll 1.* C.S., N.S., **87**. 1928. For 1401.

Ducatus Lancastriae ... pars secunda: a calendar of the pleadings etc., in the reigns of Hen. VII, Hen. VIII, Edw. VI, Queen Mary and Phil. & Mary. Record Commissioners, 1823. Bound with *pars prima.*

Ducatus Lancastriae, pars tertia: calendar of pleadings, depositions, etc. in the reigns of Henry VII, Henry VIII, Edward VI, Queen Mary, and Philip and Mary, and to the pleadings of the first thirteen years of the reign of Queen Elizabeth. Record Commissioners, 1827.

FISHWICK, HENRY, ed. *Pleadings and depositions in the Duchy court of Lancaster, time of Henry VII and Henry VIII.* L.C.R.S. 32. 1896. Covers 1489-1532.

FISHWICK, HENRY, ed. *Pleadings and depositions in the Duchy Court of Lancaster, time of Henry VIII.* L.C.R.S. 35. 1897.

FISHWICK, HENRY, ed. *Pleadings and depositions in the Duchy court of Lancaster, time of Edward VI and Philip and Mary.* L.C.R.S., 40. 1899.

Ducatus Lancastriae pars quarta: Calendar to the pleadings from the fourteenth year to the end of the reign of Queen Elizabeth. Commisioners on the Public Records, 1834.

C. *National and County Archives*

The archives of national and county government are essential sources of information for the genealogist, and many publications based on them are listed in other sections of this bibliography; for example, official lists of names are identified in section 6. Here are listed a wide range of works dealing with topics such as Quarter Sessions, charities, *quo warranto* proceedings, *etc.* Arrangement is chronological, beginning with two works which list the various courts whose records may have genealogical value:

TALLENT-BATEMAN, CHAS. T. 'The ancient Lancashire and Cheshire local courts of civil jurisdiction', 61-79. L.C.A.S. 4, 1886, 61-79.

TALLENT-BATEMAN, CHAS. T. 'The ancient Lancashire and Cheshire local courts of criminal and special jurisdiction', L.C.A.S 5, 1887, 231-41.

FARRER, W. *The Lancashire pipe rolls of 31 Henry I, A.D. 1130, and of the reigns of Henry II, A.D. 1155-1189, Richard I, A.D. 1189-99 and King John, A.D. 1199-1216.* Liverpool: Henry Young and Sons, 1902.

CANTLE, A. *The pleas of Quo Warranto for the County of Lancaster.* C.S., N.S., **98.** 1937. Includes numerous 13th c. pedigrees.

PARKER, JOHN, ed. *A calendar of the Lancashire assize rolls preserved in the Public Record Office, London.* L.C.R.S. **47 & 49.** 1904-5. 13th c.

'Some inhabitants of Salford Hundred in A.D. 1246', *L.C.A.N* 2, 1886, 102-5. Lists pledges at the Assizes.

LUMBY, J.H. 'Chester and Liverpool in the *patent rolls* of Richard II and the Lancastrian and Yorkist Kings', *H.S.L.C.* 55-6; N.S., **19-20,** 1903-4, 163-87. Includes list of men granted letters of protection to accompany Sir John Stanley in Ireland, 1386-91.

TUPLING, G.H., ed. *South Lancashire in the reign of Edward II as illustrated by the pleas at Wigan, recorded in Coram Rege roll no. 254.* C.S., 3rd series **1.** 1949.

STEWART-BROWN, R. 'Two Liverpool medieval affrays', *H.S.L.C.* **85,** 1933, 71-88. Includes list of those pardoned, 1346-7.

ANDERTON, H. INCE. 'A Blackburnshire puture roll', *H.S.L.C.* **64;** N.S., **28,** 1912, 273-86. Lists manorial lords owing feudal dues, 15th c.

'Some Lancashire offenders against the sumptuary laws in A.D. 1429', *L.C.A.N.* 2, 1886, 129-32. List.

MYERS, A.R. 'An official progress through Lancashire and Cheshire in 1476', *H.S.L.C.* **115,** 1963, 1-29. Record of a visit by the Council of the Duchy of Lancaster.

HARLAND, JOHN, ed. *The Lancashire lieutenancy under the Tudors and Stuarts: the civil and military government of the county, as illustrated by a series of royal and other letters, orders of the Privy Council, the Lord Lieutenant, and other authorities etc., etc., chiefly derived from the Shuttleworth mss at Gawthorpe Hall, Lancashire.* C.S., O.S., **49-50.** 1859. Includes muster roll, 1574.

WALLIS, JOHN EYRE WINSTANLEY. 'The narrative of the indictment of the traitors of Whalley and Cartmell, 1536-7', *Chetham miscellanies 5.* C.S., N.S., **90.** 1931. Separately paginated. Includes list of persons tried.

STEWART-BROWN, R. *Lancashire and Cheshire cases in the Court of Star Chamber.* L.C.R.S. **71**. 1916. Pt. 1. No more published. Abstracts of 108 suits.

FISHWICK, CAROLINE, ed. *A calendar of Lancashire and Cheshire Exchequer depositions by commission, from 1558 to 1702.* L.C.R.S. **11**. 1885. Includes brief description of depositions.

TODD, ANDREW A. 'Notes on sources, 9: Jury or freeholder lists', *L.* **4**(3), 1983, 7-8. In Quarter Sessions records.

'Petitions to Quarter Sessions', *Lancashire Record Office report 1963, 21-6.* Discussion, 17-20th c.

QUINTRELL, B.W., ed. *Proceedings of the Lancashire justices of the peace at the sheriffs table during assizes week, 1578-1694.* L.C.R.S., **121**. 1981.

TAIT, JAMES, ed. *Lancashire quarter sessions records.* C.S., N.S., **77**. 1917. v. 1. Quarter sessions rolls, 1590-1606. No more published in this series.

HARDY, W.J., ed. *The manuscripts of Lord Kenyon.* Historical Manuscripts Commission 14th Report, Appendix, part 4. C7571. H.M.S.O., 1894. Mainly 17th c. letters relating to county government.

EARWAKER, J.P., ed. 'Obligatory knighthood, *temp* Charles I: lists of the esquires and gentlemen in Cheshire and Lancashire who refused the order of knighthood at the coronation of Charles I drawn up in the years 1631 and 1632', in *Miscellanies relating to Lancashire and Cheshire,* **1**. L.C.R.S. **12**, 1885, 191-223.

FFARINGTON, SUSAN MARIA, ed. *The shrievalty of William Ffarington esq., A.D. 1636; documents relating to the Civil War, and an appendix containing a collection of letters taken from the Ffarington correspondence between the years 1547 and 1688.* C.S., O.S., **39**. 1856.

STANNING, J.H. *The Royalist composition papers, being the proceedings of the Committee for Compounding, A.D. 1643-1660, so far as they relate to the County of Lancaster, extracted from the records preserved in the Public Record Office, London.* 7 vols. L.C.R.S. **24, 26, 29, 36, 72, 95 & 96**. 1891-1942. The last three vols. edited by John Brownbill.

ABRAM, W.A. 'Lancashire royalists whose estates were sequestrated in 1652', *L.C.A.N.* **1**, 1885, 88-91. List.

'Sir Roger Bradshaigh's letter-book', *H.S.L.C.* **63**; N.S., **27**, 1911, 120-73. Lieutenancy papers, 1660-76.

BEAMONT, WILLIAM, ed. *The Jacobite trials at Manchester in 1694.* C.S., O.S., **28**. 1853.

PORTEUS, T.C. 'New light on the Lancashire Jacobite plot, 1692-4', *L.C.A.S.* **50**, 1934-5, 1-64. Includes transcripts of documents, giving many names.

DELACY, MARGARET. *Prison reform in Lancashire 1700-1850: a study in local administration.* C.S., 3rd series, **33**. 1986. Includes useful list of sources.

TAYLOR, PETER. 'Quarter sessions in Lancashire in the middle of the eighteenth century: the court in session and its records', *H.S.L.C.* **139**, 1990, 63-82.

'Removals of Cumbrians', *C.F.H.S.N.* **43**, 1987, 8. From Lancashire to Cumberland and Westmorland, 18th c. From the index to Quarter session records at Preston.

'Evidence of illegitimacy in early Manchester newspapers', *M.G.* **17**(1), 1981, 7-9. Lists recognizances entered into in bastardy cases from the *Manchester Mercury* 1780-1800', **17**(2), 1981, 41-3.

'Peter Loo massacre, 16 August 1819', *M.G.* **4**(2), 1968 15-16. List of persons wounded.

'Peterloo', *M.G.* **25**(3), 1989, 4-13. Lists persons wounded and imprisoned at this famous meeting of Manchester radicals; also lists magistrates and Yeomanry.

The reports of the Commissioners ... to enquire concerning charities in England and Wales relating to the County of Lancashire 1819-1837. P.S. King & Son, 1890

MARSHALL, J.D., ed. *The history of Lancashire County Council, 1889-1974.* Martin Robertson, 1977. Scholarly; includes biographical notes on chairmen and other officers.

10. RECORDS OF LOCAL ADMINISTRATION

The records of borough, parochial and township government — churchwardens' accounts, rate lists, poor law records, etc., contain a great deal of information valuable to the genealogist. Those which have been published are listed here.

Balderstone
See Osbaldestone

Barrow
HARRISON, BRETT. 'Sources for family history in Barrow-inFurness', *C.F.H.S.N.* **17**, 1980, 19. Brief note on parish records.

Biggar
PEARSON, H. GARENCIERES. 'The town's book of Biggar, Isle of Walney', *C.W.A.A.S.Tr.* N.S., **11**, 1911, 185-98. General discussion with some extracts.

Blackburn
'St.Paul's, Blackburn: churchwarden's account book, 1751', *L.* **1**(6), 1976, 107-14; **1**(7), 1976, 127-34; **1**(8), 1976, 147-154.
'Blackburn churchwardens' accounts book, 1753 [and 1754]', *L.* **1**(2), 1975, 29-32; **1**(3), 1975, 47-54; **1**(4), 1975, 67-74; **1**(5), 1976, 87-94. Extracts.

Blackburn Hundred
'A High Constable's register, 1681', *H.S.L.C.* **107**, 1955, 55-87. Register of Ambrose Barcroft, high constable of Blackburn Hundred.

Bolton
ARKWRIGHT, KATHLEEN. *An alphabetical index to the poor rate assessment book of the parish of Bolton-le-Moors, 1686.* [Bolton: Bolton Libraries,] 1986.
G., J.D. 'Early subscribers to the free library building', in BARTON, B.T., ed. *Historical gleanings of Bolton and District [first series].* Bolton: Daily Chronicle Office, 1881, 192-9. List, 1824, with biographical notes.

'Bolton county magistrates from 1750 to 1875', in BARTON, B.T., ed. *Historical gleanings of Bolton and District [first series].* Bolton: Daily Chronicle Office, 1881, 35. List.
'Boroughreeves and constables of Bolton', in BARTON, B.T., ed. *Historical gleanings of Bolton and District [first series].* Bolton: Daily Chronicle Office, 1881, 33-34. List. 1801-39.
'The charities of Bolton', in BARTON, B.T., ed. *Historical gleanings of Bolton and District [second series].* Bolton: Daily Chronicle Office, 1882, 131-67. Includes much information on benefactors.
'Early trustees of Great Bolton', in BARTON. B.T., ed. *Historical gleanings of Bolton and District [first series].* Bolton: Daily Chronicle Office, 1881, 28-9. List 1792-1841.
Index for poor rate assessment book, Great Bolton, 1805. 1 fiche. [Bolton]: B.D.F.H.S., 1985.

Bury
TODD, ANDREW A. 'Notes on sources 2: terriers', *L.* **3**(8), 1981, 14-16; **3**(9), 1982, 15-17; **3**(10), 1982, 15-17. Terrier of Bury, 1696.
TODD, ANDREW A. 'Notes on sources 7: Bury select vestry overseers' minutes 1823-30', *L.* **4**(1), 1983, 9-10.
'Examinations of the poor of Bury', *M.G.* Spring 1975, 13-15; **11**(2), 1975, 16-17. 18-19th c.
'Settlement and removal in Bury, 1679-82', *Lancashire Record Office report* 1958, 14-21.

Bury Union
'The Bury Union indenture book, 1812-1844', *L.* **1**(5), 1976, 97-100. Lists apprentices and their masters.

Butterworth
See Castleton

Cartmel Fell
JONES, G.P., & MACPHERSON, SHEILA J. 'Cartmel Fell parish church documents', *C.W.A.A.S.Tr.* N.S., **66**, 1966 220-47. Includes a list of documents, many abstracts, and lists of constables and graves, overseers, chapelwardens, etc., mainly 18th c.

Castleton

GORDON, R.J. 'First assessment lists for the townships of Castleton (1759), the Lordship side of Butterworth (1763) and the township of Spotland (1750)', *Transactions of the Rochdale Literary and Scientific Society* **12**, 1914-16, 17-28. For the poor-lay.

Chorlton on Medlock

'Overseers of Chorlton-on-Medlock, 1714-1770', *L.G.* **2**, 1877 35-6. List of overseers.

Clitheroe

HARLAND, JOHN, ed. *Ancient charters and other muniments of the Borough of Clithero in the County Palatine of Lancaster.* [Clitheroe]: The Corporation, 1851. Not many names.

Culcheth

BULMER, J.R., ed. *Culcheth workhouse 1834-1836.* 1 fiche. [Liverpool]: Liverpool and S.W. Lancashire F.H.S., 1988. List of paupers.

NORBURY, W. 'Churchwardens for Culcheth 1678-1758', *L.C.A.N.* **1**, 1885, 102-4. List.

NORBURY, W. 'Overseers of the poor for Culcheth, 1668-1770', *L.C.A.N.* **1**, 1885, 156, 225-6. List, actually to 1776.

NORBURY, W. 'Township constables of Culcheth', *L.C.A.N.* **1**, 1885, 21-2, 40-41 & 54-6. List, 1665-1776.

Dalton

KELLY, PAUL V. 'An inventory of the parish chest at Dalton church', *C.W.A.A.S.Tr.* N.S., **36**, 1936, 100-103.

Didsbury

'[Tithe apportionments]', *Cheshire family historian* **5**, 1975, 18-19. Includes apportionment for Didsbury, 1845.

Downholland

'Downholland township records', *Lancashire Record Office report* 1974, 20-22,

Droylsden

'Droylsden landowners, 1805', *M.G.* **20**(1) 1984, 13-14. List from a map of Droylsden highways.

Farnworth

MADELEY, CHARLES. 'Roll of the mock corporation of Farnworth in Widnes', *H.S.L.C.* **67**; N.S., **31**, 1915, 27-77. Records of a social club, listing many members.

Garstang

HUGHES, T. CANN. 'Notes on the Garstang Trust and their records', *L.C.A.S.* **30**, 1912, 164-77. Includes list of bailiffs, 1801-84.

Goosnargh

BANISTER, E.D. 'The vestry book of the twenty-four sworne men of Goosnargh', *H.S.L.C.* **50**; N.S., **14**, 1898, 41-64. General discussion, not a transcript.

Great Sankey

DUNLOP, G.A., & RIDEOUT, ERIC H. 'The township papers of Great Sankey, Lancashire', *H.S.L.C.* **84**, 1932, 91-125. Includes folded list of constables and overseers, and of supervisors of the highway, 1698-1779, lists of removal orders and apprenticeship indentures, militia returns 1798, 1802 and 1807.

Halliwell

SPARKE, ARCHIBALD, ed. *The township booke of Halliwell.* C.S., N.S., **69**. 1910. 1640-1762.

Hawkshead

WILKINSON, S. 'Hawkeshead paupers', *C.F.H.S.N.* **53**, 1989, 14-15. List, 1814.

Huyton.

CROOKS, FREDERIC. 'Huyton church-wardens 1783-1834', *H.S.L.C.* **90**, 1938, 177-9. List.

Kirkham

SHAW, R. CUNLIFFE, & SHAW, HELEN G. *The records of the thirty men of the parish of Kirkham in Lancashire, And the history of Kirkham Grammar School from A.D. 1621-1663, with extracts from the bailiffs book and an account of the Clifton and Westby quires in the parish church written about 1663.* Kendal: Titus Wilson & Son, 1930.

Lancaster

BROWNBILL, JOHN. *A calendar of charters and records belonging to the Corporation of Lancaster,* arranged by John R. Nuttall. Lancaster: the Corporation, 1929.

PAPE, THOMAS. *The charters of the city of Lancaster.* Lancaster: Lancaster City Council, 1952.

'Early mayors of Lancaster', *H.S.L.C.* 63; N.S., 27, 1911, 174-7. See also 66; N.S., 30, 1914, 266-7, & 67; N.S., 31, 1915, 166. Medieval-17th c. list.

HUGHES, T. CANN, ed. *The rolls of the freemen of the Borough of Lancaster, 1688 to 1840,* transcribed by W.B. Kendall. L.C.R.S., 87 & 90. 1935-8.

Leigh

PINK, WM. DUNCOMBE. *Leigh municipal record, 1863-1907.* Leigh: The Corporation, 1907. Record of local council elections, with some biographical notes.

Little Bolton

Index for poor rate assessment book, Little Bolton, 1831. 1 fiche. [Bolton]: B.D.F.H.S., 1985.

Liverpool

MORTON, T.N. 'A concise account of the charters, muniments, and other records of the Corporation of Liverpool, in the year 1897', *H.S.L.C.* 49. N.S., 8, 1898, 71-86.

PICTON, JAMES A. *The City of Liverpool: selections from the municipal archives and records, from the 13th to the 17th century inclusive.* Liverpool: Gilbert G. Walmsley, 1883.

PICTON, JAMES A., SIR, et al. 'Notes on the charters of the Borough (now city) of Liverpool', *H.S.L.C.* 36, 1884, 53-128. Includes many names.

ELTON, JOHN. 'Early recorded mayors of Liverpool: an original list with documentary authorities', *H.S.L.C.* 53; N.S., 18, 1902, 119-30. Medieval.

STEWART-BROWN, R. *The inhabitants of Liverpool from the 14th to the 18th century.* Liverpool: privately printed, 1930. Transcripts of subsidy and other tax rolls, burgess rolls, the protestation 1641-2, parish assessments, *etc.*

HANCE, EDWARD M., & MORTON, T.N. 'The burgess rolls of Liverpool during the 16th century', *H.S.L.C.* 35, 1883, 14786. Includes biographical notes.

PLATT, E.M. 'Extracts from the Liverpool Corporation records, 1541-1701', *H.S.L.C.,* 55-6; N.S., 19-20, 1903-4, 90-106. Dealing with shipping, apprenticeships, indentures and parliamentary elections.

PLATT, E.M. 'Further extracts from the Liverpool Corporation records, 1541-1701', *H.S.L.C.,* 55-6; N.S., 19-20, 1903-4, 188-208. Notes on municipal officers.

TWEMLOW, J.A., ed. *Liverpool town books: proceedings of assemblies, common councils, portmoot courts, etc., 1550-1862.* 2 vols. Liverpool: University Press, 1918-35. v. 1. 1550-1571. v. 2. 1571-1603. No more published. Extensive.

HANCE, EDWARD M., & MORTON, T.N. 'The burgess rolls of Liverpool during the 17th century', *H.S.L.C.* 36, 1884, 12958. Includes biographical notes.

CHANDLER, GEORGE. *Liverpool under Charles I.* Liverpool: Brown, Picton and Hornby Libraries, 1965. Includes extensive transcript of *Liverpool town book under Charles I: proceedings of the Borough Council,* ed. E.K. Wilson.

SAXTON, E.B. 'Losses of the inhabitants of Liverpool on the taking of the town in 1644', *H.S.L.C.* 91, 1939, 181-91. Lists 357 persons, and the value of their losses when Prince Rupert took Liverpool in 1645.

CHANDLER, GEORGE. *Liverpool under James I.* Liverpool: Brown, Picton and Hornby Libraries, 1960. Includes extensive transcript of the *Liverpool town book under James I,* ed. E.B. Saxton.

PEET, HENRY, ed. *Liverpool vestry books 1681-1834.* 2 vols. Liverpool: University Press, 1912-15. v. 1. 1681-1799. v. 2. 1800-1834, with supplementary extracts 1835-1842.

BLEASE, W. LYON. 'The poor law in Liverpool, 1681-1834', *H.S.L.C.* 61; N.S. 25, 1909, 97-182.

PEET, HENRY. *Liverpool in the reign of Queen Anne, 1705-1708, from a rate assessment book of the town and parish, with an appendix containing inscriptions* from the monuments and windows of the parish churches and abstracts of several wills. Liverpool: Henry Young & Sons, 1908.

PEET, HENRY. 'Liverpool in the reign of Queen Anne, 1705 and 1708, from a rate assessment book of the town and parish, giving one of the earliest known lists of inhabitants, with their respective holdings, according to streets', *H.S.L.C.* **59**; N.S., **23**, 1907, appendix 1-177. Also includes monumental inscriptions and will abtracts.

'Liverpool Workhouse records collection', *L.F.H.S.J.* **2**(1), 1978, 8-11. Calendar of archives.

MCCANN, JO. 'Cholera', *L.F.H.* **15**(1), 1993, 4-6. Discusses a report of the Medical Officer of Health for Liverpool, 1866, which lists deaths from cholera.

WHITE, BRIAN D. *A history of the corporation of Liverpool, 1835-1914.* Liverpool: University Press, 1951.

Manchester

REDFORD, ARTHUR. *The history of local government in Manchester.* 3 vols. Longman Green and Co., 1939-40. v. 1. Manor and township. v. 2. Borough and city. v. 3. The last half century. General study.

AXON, E.A., ed. 'Documents relating to the plague in Manchester in 1605 with other memoranda, 1593-1606', in *Chetham miscellanies,* N.S., **3**. C.S., N.S., **73**, 1915, separately paginated. Notes many names.

AXON, ERNEST, ed. *Manchester sessions: notes of proceedings before Oswald Mosley (1616-1630), Nicholas Mosley (1661-1672), and Sir Oswald Mosley (1734-1739), and other magistrates.* L.C.R.S. **42**. 1901. v. 1. 1616-1622/23. No more published. Includes brief pedigree of Moseley, 17-18th c., list of justices of the peace, 1615-16, etc.

EARWAKER, J.P., ed. *The Constables' accounts of the manor of Manchester from the year 1612 to the year 1647, and from the year 1743 to the year 1776.* Manchester: Henry Blacklock and Co., 1891-2.

BROXAP, ERNEST, ed. 'A Manchester assessment of 1648', in *Chetham miscellanies* N.S. **2**; C.S., N.S., **63**. 1909, separately paginated.

BROXAP, ERNEST, ed. 'Extracts from the Manchester churchwardens accounts 1664-1710', *Chetham miscellanies* N.S., **4**; C.S., N.S., **80**, 1921, separately paginated.

'John Hartley, J.P., of Strangeways Hall, Manchester, and his fellow townsmen', *P.N.* **3**, 1883, 37-42. See also 95-7, & **4**, 1884, 87-90. Reprinted with corrections in *M.G.* **27**(3), 1991, 3-8. Includes list of 341 Mancunians who petitioned to remove Hartley as a J.P., 1675 (or later?)

'Manchester subscribers to a fund for raising troops, 1745', *P.N.* **3**, 1883, 235-6. List.

HINDLE, G.B. *Provision for the relief of the poor in Manchester 1754-1826.* C.S. 3rd series **22**. 1975. General study of the poor law; includes useful bibliography.

SPIERS, MAURICE. *Victoria Park, Manchester: a nineteenth century suburb in its social and administrative context.* C.S. 3rd series **23**. 1976. Includes list of prominent residents, 19th c.

HARRISON, WILLIAM. 'The old house of correction at Hunt's Bank, Manchester', *L.C.A.S.* **3**, 1885, 89-110.

'Manchester rate book districts', *M.G.* **17**(2) 1981, 44-5.

North Meols

BRAY, DOUG. 'Nineteenth century North Meols removal orders', *L.F.A.* **9**(1), 1987, 4-8. List.

RIDEOUT, ERIC HARDWICKE. 'Poor law administration in North Meols in the eighteenth century', *H.S.L.C.* **81**, 1929, 62-109. Includes lists of settlement certificates, removal orders, bastardy orders, and apprenticeship indentures, *etc.*

Oldham

List of members of the Oldham Town Council since the date of the incorporation of the borough one the 13th June 1849, to the 31st December, 1924 ... Oldham: County Borough of Oldham, 1924.

Osbaldestone

ABRAM, W.A. 'A valuation of the townships of Osbaldestone and Balderstone made in 1712', *L.C.A.N.* **2**, 1886, 23-4.

Prescot

BAILEY, F.A., ed. *The churchwardens' accounts of Prescot, Lancashire, 1523-1607.* L.C.R.S., **104**. 1953. Lists fees paid for burials, thus supplementing the parish register.

BAILEY, F.A., ed. 'The churchwardens' accounts of Prescot, 1523-1607.' *H.S.L.C.* **92**, 1940, 133-201; **95**, 1943, 1-30. Discussion with many extracts; includes the will of Gilbert Latham, 1552.

CLAPHAM, J.H. 'Tithe surveys as a source of agrarian history', *Cambridge historical journal* **1**(2), 1923-5, 201. 8. Discussion of the survey for Prescot, 1775.

Prestbury

KNOWLES, RICHARD E. 'Old time punishment and the restoration of the Prestbury stocks', *L.C.A.S.* **54**, 1939, 143-56. Includes 17th c. extracts from Wigan court leet rolls, *etc.*

Preston

ABRAM, W. ALEXANDER, ed. *The rolls of burgesses at the Guilds Merchant of the Borough of Preston, Co. Lancaster 1397-1682.* L.C.R.S. **9**. 1884.

ABRAM, W. A. *Memorials of the Preston guilds, illustrating the manner in which the Guild Merchant has been held in the Borough from the earliest on record until the last guild in 1862 ...* Preston: George Toulmin, 1882. Many names, but unfortunately no index.

CHEETHAM, F.H. 'Bell ringing orders at Preston church, 1587-8', *H.S.L.C.* **78**; N.S., **42**, 1926, 130-35. Lists leading parishioners.

DOBSON, WILLIAM, & HARLAND, JOHN. *A history of Preston guild & the ordinances of various guilds merchant, the custumal of Preston, the charters to the borough, the incorporated companies, list of mayors from 1327, etc., etc.* Preston: W. & J. Dobson, 1862.

HEWITSON, A. *Preston town-council, or, portraits of local legislators, together with a list of all the mayors, aldermen and councillors elected for the Borough of Preston between 1835 and 1870.* Preston: Chronicle Office, 1870.

PARKER, R.D. 'The changing character of Preston Guild Merchant, 1762-1862', *Northern history* **20**, 1984, 108-26. The Guild Merchant was a festival held every twenty years.

POLLARD, WILLIAM. *A descriptive narrative of the Guild Merchant of Preston in the County Palatine of Lancaster as celebrated in the year 1882.* Preston: H. Oakey, 1883. Many names.

RICHARDSON, LAWRENCE B. 'Notes on sources **3**: Preston guild rolls', *L.* **3**(9), 1982, 8-9.

RICHARDSON, LAWRENCE B. 'Any Preston area connections?' *C.F.H.S.N.* **22**, 1982, 3-4. Discusses the potential of Preston guild records.

SMITH, TOM C. *A popular history of Preston Guild, from the earliest times down to the year 1902, with a concise guide to the borough of Preston and district.* Preston: Alfred Halewood, 1902.

WILCOCKSON, I. *Authentic records of the Guild Merchant of Preston in the County Palatine of Lancaster in the year 1822 ...* Preston: I. Wilcockson, et al, 1822. Many names.

Preston Union

PROCTOR, WINIFRED. Poor Law administration in Preston Union, 1838-1848', *H.S.L.C.* **117**, 1965, 145-66. General discussion.

Ribchester

'The aggrieved parishioner of Ribchester', 1639', *P.N.* **3**, 1883, 43-5. Concerns a dispute over the choice of a church-warden; includes names of leading parishioners.

Rochdale

COLE, JOHN. *Down Poorhouse Lane: the diary of a Rochdale workhouse.* Littleborough: Kelsall, 1984. Diary covers 1836-45.

EARWAKER, J.P. 'The mock corporation of Rochdale', *H.S.L.C.* **40**; N.S., **4**, 1888, 93-120. Records of a social club, 18th c., many names.

Salford

MANDLEY, J.G. de T., ed. *The portmote or court leet records of the borough or town and royal manor of Salford from the year 1597 to the year 1669 inclusive.* C.S., N.S., 46 & 48. 1902.

TAIT, JAMES. 'Records of some Salford port moots in the sixteenth century', *Chetham miscellanies* N.S., 4 C.S., N.S., 80, 1921, separately paginated

'The poor people of Salford', *M.G.* Autumn 1973, 9-10; Winter 1973-4, 5-6. Extracts from Overseers' accounts, 1797-8.

Salford Union

'Unfilmed 1851 census of Manchester, Salford and districts', *M.G.* 31(1), 1995, 46-7. Schedule for Salford Union workhouse.

Sefton

HORLEY, ENGELBERT. 'The mock corporation of Sephton', *H.S.L.C.* 33, 1881, 223-46; 34, 1883, 25-38. Includes list of mock mayors, *etc.*, 1780-1809.

SAXTON, EVELINE B. 'Early records of the mock corporation of Sefton', *H.S.L.C.* 100, 1943, 73-89.

Spotland

See Castleton

Sutton

'List of all men in Sutton (near Warrington) aged between 18-45 on 3 March 1792, by Richard Mainwaring, constable', *Family History Society of Cheshire journal* 6(1), 1976, 6.

Ulverston

LACE, PETER R. 'At Ulverston', *C.F.H.S.N.* 57, 1990, 16-18. Extensive list of clergy, merchants and tradesmen, etc., who attended a public meeting at Ulverston, 1848.

West Derby Hundred

OXLEY, G.W. 'The permanent poor in South-West Lancashire under the old poor law', in HARRIS, J.R., ed. *Liverpool and Merseyside: essays in the economic and social history of the port and its hinterland.* Frank Cass & Co., 1969, 16-49. General study based on records of the parishes and townships in West Derby Hundred.

Westhoughton

TODD, MARJORIE. 'Churchwardens of the township of Westhoughton', *M.G.* 19(2), 1983, 39. 1723-1839.

Wigan

CLARE, J. LEIGH. 'An account of certificates given to persons within this town and parish of Wigan, to be touched for the King's evil by King James the Second at Chester city', *H.S.L.C.* 1, 1848, 26. List, 1687.

The charters of the ancient and royal borough of Wigan. Wigan: Wigan Education Committee, 1960. Not many names.

See also Prestbury

Worsley

MULLINEUX, C.E. *Pauper and poorhouse: a study of the administration of the poor laws in a Lancashire parish.* Pendlebury: Swinton and Pendlebury Public Libraries, 1966. Concerns Worsley; general study.

POLLARD, MARJORIE. 'Jurors lists', *M.G.* 22(1), 1986 9-10. Includes list of those qualified to serve in 1830 from Worsley.

11. ECCLESIASTICAL RECORDS

A. *Church of England, etc.*

The role of the church in pre-industrial England was much wider than it is today. This fact is reflected in the wide range of ecclesiastical records available to the genealogist. Some of these − parish registers, probate records, churchwardens' accounts, *etc.* − are dealt with in other sections of this book. This section focuses on those records and studies which are more directly concerned with ecclesiastical administration. From the sixteenth to the nineteenth century, Lancashire formed part of the diocese of Chester. Its records are discussed in:

THACKER, A.T. 'Chester Diocesan records and the local historian', *H.S.L.C.* **130**, 1981, 149-85. Since 1541.

See also:

'The records of the Western deaneries of the Archdeaconry of Richmond', *Lancashire Record Office report* 1954, 10-16.

Prior to the Reformation, Lancashire was in the Archdiocese of York. The records of the Archdiocese includes numerous references to Lancashire; see, for example:

BROWN, WILLIAM, ed. *The register of William Greenfield, Lord Archbishop of York, 1306-1315.* Surtees Society **145, 149, & 151-3.** 1931-40.

Registers of other Archbishops of York also contain some material relating to Lancashire; in due course, those which have been published will be listed in the Yorkshire volume of *British genealogical bibliographies.*

A number of works provide evidence regarding the state of the church at the Reformation; these record many names:

HAIGH, CHRISTOPHER. *The last days of the Lancashire monasteries and the Pilgrimage of Grace.* C.S., 3rd series **17.** 1969. Includes lists of monks at the surpression, and purchasers of monastic lands.

BAILEY, JOHN EGLINGTON, ed. *Inventories of goods in the churches and chapels of Lancashire, taken in the year A.D. 1552.*

C.S., O.S., **107 & 113.** 1879-88; N.S., **47,** 1902. Chetham miscellanies, N.S., **1,** separately paginated. Pt. 1 Salford Hundred. Pt. 2. West Derby, Blackburn and Leyland Hundreds. Pt. 3. Amounderness and Lonsdale Hundreds. Many names of churchwardens *etc.*

RAINES, F.R., ed. *A history of the chantries within the County Palatine of Lancaster, being the reports of the royal commisioners of Henry VIII, Edward VI and Queen Mary.* C.S., O.S. **59-60.** 1862. Gives names of founders, many rentals, *etc.*

IRVINE, WM. FERGUSSON. 'Church discipline in the sixteenth century, as shown by extracts from the Bishop of Chester's ms. visitation books for the Deanery of Manchester', *L.C.A.S.* **13,** 1895, 56-69.

'The state, civil and ecclesiastical, of the County of Lancaster, about the year 1590', in *Chetham miscellanies,* **5**; C.S., O.S., **96,** 1875, separately paginated. Puritan tract including biographical notes on 17 puritan preachers, and the will of John Buckley of Manchester, 1593.

For ordinations, presentations and institutions, see:

SOMERVILLE, ROBERT. 'Duchy of Lancaster presentations 1399-1485', *Bulletin of the Institute of Historical Research* **18,** 1941, 52-76.

IRVINE, WM. FERGUSSON, ed. 'The earliest ordination book of the Diocese of Chester, 1542-7 & 1555-8', in *Miscellanies relating to Lancashire and Cheshire* **4.** L.C.R.S. **43,** 1902, separately paginated.

GRIGSON, FRANCIS. 'Institutions to Lancashire and Cheshire livings', *L.C.A.N.* **1,** 1885, 92-6, 111-6, 196-8, 203-5, 214-20 & 228-34; **2,** 1886, 24-6, 3741, 67-79 & 113-26. Lists clergy, 17th c.

A number of records of clerical taxation have been published; these give names of clergy, and include:

BENNET, M.J. 'The Lancashire and Cheshire clergy, 1379', *H.S.L.C.* **124,** 1972, 1-30. Includes transcript of the clerical poll-tax returns for the Archdeaconry of Chester, 1379, listing clergy.

MCNULTY, JOSEPH. 'Religious in North Lancashire, 1380-1', *L.C.A.S.* **54**, 1939, 207-8. Names from a clerical subsidy roll.

IRVINE, WM. FERGUSSON, 'A list of the clergy in the eleven deaneries of the Diocese of Chester, 1541-42, together with a list of the tenths and subsidy payable in ten deaneries [circa 1538]', in *Miscellanies relating to Lancashire and Cheshire* 3. L.C.R.S. **33**, 1896, separately paginated.

BRIDGEMAN, G.T.O., ed. 'Loans, contributions, subsidies and ship money paid by the clergy of the Diocese of Chester in the years 1620, 1622, 1624, 1634, 1635, 1636 and 1639 (as recorded in the private ledger of John Bridgeman, D.D. Bishop of Chester ...)', in *Miscellanies relating to Lancashire and Cheshire* 1. L.C.R.S. **12**. 1885, 43-129.

A number of publications provide lists of clergy:

AXON, ERNEST. 'The King's preachers in Lancashire, 1599-1845', *L.C.A.S.* **56**, 1941-2, 67-104. Biographical notes on many clergy.

BROWNBILL, JOHN, ed. 'List of clergymen etc., in the Diocese of Chester, 1691 recorded at the first visitation of Nicholas Stratford, Bishop of Chester', *Chetham miscellanies* N.S., 3 C.S, N.S., **73**, 1915, separately paginated.

D[REDGE], J.I. 'The nonjurors of the Diocese of Chester', *P.N.* **2**, 1882, 238-40. Lists clergy refusing the oath of allegiance to William III.

'A list of the established churches in Manchester, Salford, etc., ...', *M.G.* **25**(1), 1989, 6-8. Lists clergy of both Anglican and nonconformist churches, 1836.

The Liverpool Diocesan calendar ... Liverpool: Church Press, 1881- . Title varies. Includes list of clergy and names of churchwardens, *etc.*

The study of church bells may be useful to the genealogist. Bell founders, clergy, churchwardens and benefactors are all mentioned in:

CHEETHAM, F.H. 'The church bells of Lancashire', *L.C.A.S.* **32**, 1914, 1-163; **33**, 1915, 1-116; **34**, 1916, 1-76; **35**, 1917, 109-20; **37**, 1919, 35-66; **38**, 1920, 87-111; **39**, 1921, 125-81; **40**, 1922-3, 76-153; **45**, 1928, 89-128. See also:

HAWKES, ARTHUR J. 'An addendum on the Wigan bellfounders', *L.C.A.S.* **58**, 1945-6, 241-4. Especially concerns Ashton and Scott families.

The Diocese of Manchester was founded in the nineteenth century. For its history, see:

DOBB, ARTHUR J. *Like a mighty tortoise: a history of the Diocese of Manchester.* Manchester: [the author,] 1978. Includes a survey of the parishes in the diocese.

Bailey
NEWDIGATE, C.A. 'The chantry of St. John Baptist at Bailey', *H.S.L.C.* **68**; N.S., **32**, 1916, 118-58. Includes list of chantry priests. Also notes on the families of Cliderow and Shireburn.

Bispham
'The inhabitants of Bispham parish, 1676', *Fylde Historical and Antiquarian Society [journal]* **1**, 1940, 47-53. List probably made for an ecclesiastical visitation.

Blackburn
WALLIS, JOHN EYRE WINSTANLEY. *A history of the church in Blackburnshire.* S.P.C.K., 1932.

Blackley
'Platform at Blackley Chapel (c. 17th century)', *M.G.* **26**(1), 1990, 17. Plan of seat holders.

Bolton
D., J.G. 'Improvements in the old parish church at Bolton', in BARTON, B.T., ed. *Historical gleanings of Bolton and District [third series].* Bolton: Daily Chronicle Office, 1883, 329-35. Notes on those concerned with them, c.1795.

'A short history of St. Peter's church, Bolton-le-Moors: Bolton parish church', *M.G.* **24**(1), 1988, 29-33. Includes list of vicars, 12-20th c.

Burtonwood
'Burtonwood Chapel: a communal effort in church building and education', *Lancashire Record Office report* 1966, 47-55. Discussion of its records.

Childwall
'Pew-holders in Childwall church, 1609', *H.S.L.C.* 43-4; N.S., **8-9**, 1891-2, 327-8.

Chorley
WILSON, JOHN. *Chorley church: the story of the old parish church of Chorley in Lancashire.* Edinburgh: Ballantyne Press, 1914. Includes list of clergy, pedigrees of Standish of Duxbury, Chorley of Chorley and Charnock of Charnock, and many other names.

Darwen
POMFRET, JOSEPH. *History of Holy Trinity church, Darwen: a centenary souvenir, 1829-1929.* Darwen: News Office, 1929. Includes lists of clergy, churchwardens, etc.

Deane
'Vicars of Deane', in BARTON, B.T., ed. *Historical gleanings of Bolton and District [first series].* Bolton: Daily Chronicle Office, 1881, 42. See also 75-6. List, 1471-1877.

Ellenbrook
AXON, ERNEST. 'Ellenbrook Chapel and its 17th century ministers', *L.C.A.S.* **38**, 1920, 1-34. In Eccles parish. Ministerial biographies.

Everton
MOULD, R.F. *The iron church: a short history of Everton, its mother church, and one of its mid-Victorian churchwardens, including notes on how to start tracing a family tree.* Liverpool: Everton St. George Press, 1977. Includes pedigrees of Mould, 16-20th c.

Furness
GAYTHORPE, HARPER. 'A bishop's visitation to Furness in 1554', *C.W.A.A.S.Tr.* N.S., **7**, 1907, 269-73.

Halsall
IRVINE, WM. FERGUSSON. 'Ecclesiastical memoranda as to Halsall', *H.S.L.C.* **48**; N.S., **12**; 1896, 241-52. Lists clergy, 13-19th c.

Halton
HUGHES, THOMAS CANN. 'Notes on the rectors of Halton, Lancashire, since the Commonwealth, *L.C.A.S.* **43**, 1926, 62-71.

Huyton
CROOKS, FREDERIC. 'Notes on Huyton', *H.S.L.C.* **88**, 1936, 241-7. Lists churchwardens, 1721-82, and pew-holders, 1761.

Lancaster
ROPER, WILLIAM OLIVER. *Materials for the history of the church of Lancaster.* C.S., N.S., **26, 31** & **48-9**. 1892-1906. v. 1-2. Chartulary of Lancaster Priory and related documents. v. 3 includes extracts from church books, 17-19th c., and extracts from the parish registers. v. 4 is primarily devoted to monumental inscriptions, with a list of priors, vicars, organists, parish clerks, and churchwardens.

Langho
ABRAM, WILLIAM ALEXANDER. 'The parochial chapel of St. Leonard, Langho, in Billington', *H.S.L.C.* **27**; 3rd series **3**, 1875, 33-50. Includes lists of perpetual curates 1620-1868, and of subscribers to the augmentation of the living, 1749.

Lees
HIGSON, C.E. 'Further notes on Lees chapel', *L.C.A.S.* **48**, 1932, 117-32. Bequests of pews, notes on monumental inscriptions, etc.

Liverpool
COTTON, VERE E. *The book of Liverpool Cathedral.* Liverpool: Liverpool University Press for the Liverpool Cathedral Committee, 1964. Includes lists of contributions of over £50 to 1963; also various other names.
COTTON, VERE E. *The Liverpool Cathedral official handbook.* 6th ed. Liverpool: Littlebury Bros., 1926. Includes extensive list of subscriptions to the various Cathedral building funds paid and promised to 23rd March 1926.

PEET, HENRY. 'Abstracts of deeds relating to the sale of pews in St. Nicholas's Church, Liverpool', *H.S.L.C.* **73**; N.S., **37**, 1921, 215-24. 17-18th c.

THOM, D. 'Liverpool churches and chapels: their destruction, removal, or alteration, with notices of clergymen, ministers and others', *H.S.L.C.* **4**, 1852, 137-88; **5**, 1853, 3-56. Both Anglican and Nonconformist.

Maghull

CHEETHAM, F.H. 'Maghull chapel', *H.S.L.C.* **74**; N.S., **33**, 1923, 1-67. Includes many extracts from chapel wardens' accounts, 18th c., also list of registers, a few monumental inscriptions, list of chapel wardens, 1681-1716, *etc.*

Manchester

AXON, ERNEST. 'The rectors and deans of Manchester prior to the collegiation of the parish church in 1421', *Chetham miscellanies* N.S. **6**. C.S. N.S. **94**, 1935, separately paginated. Biographies.

HIBBERT-WARE, SAMUEL. *The ancient parish church of Manchester, and why it was collegiated.* Manchester: Thomas Agnew, 1848. Includes notes on medieval clergy.

HUDSON, HY. A. 'A list of the wardens of the college of Manchester, with remarks upon an old ms. catalogue and an early printed list', *L.C.A.S.* **33**, 1915, 178-91. Wardens of the collegiate church; includes folded list, 15-20th c.

RAINES, F.R. *The fellows of the Collegiate Church of Manchester.* C.S., N.S. **21 & 23**. 1891. Biographies of clergy.

RAINES, F.R. *The rectors of Manchester, and the wardens of the collegiate church of that town.* C.S., N.S., **5-6** 1885. Includes biographies.

Cathedral and parish church of Manchester: a list of churchwardens from 1422 to 1911. Manchester: Sherrat and Hughes, 1911.

'Petition for St. Johns Church, Deansgate, 1796', *P.N.* **4**, 1884, 81-83. Includes list of Mancunian petitioners.

Oldham

'The names of strangers who have preacht at Oldham synce Easter 1665', *P.N.* **4**, 1884, 54-6. List of preachers, 1665-71.

Ormskirk

DIXON, JAMES. 'The burial list of the Ormskirk clergy and ministers', *H.S.L.C.* **29**; 3rd series **5**, 1877, 125-38. Extracts from the parish register, 16-19th c., with biographical notes.

'Ormskirk parish magazine', *O.D.F.H.* **5**, 1993, 24-6; **6**, 1993, 15-18; **7**, 1994, 2-6; **8**, 1994, 2-3. Lists names mentioned, etc. 1887-1900.

Preston

SMITH, TOM C. *Records of the parish church of Preston in Amounderness.* Preston: C.W. Whitehead, 1892. Includes transcript of the parish register, 1611-32, with extracts to 1752, biographical notes on clergy, list of churchwardens 16-18th c., *etc., etc.*

Prestwich

RAINES, F.R. 'A close catalogue of the rectors of Prestwich from 1316 to 1632, extracted from the episcopal registers of Lichfield and Chester', *Chetham miscellanies* **6**. C.S., O.S., **103**, 1878, separately paginated.

Rochdale

COUPE, JOHN. 'Rochdale chapels & churches', *M.G.* **29**(1), 1993, 13. List with dates of opening.

RAINES, F.R. *The vicars of Rochdale*, ed. Henry H. Howorth. C.S., N.S. **1-2**. 1883. Includes extensive biographical notes.

Salford

BARBER, J.J. *A history of the church of the Sacred Trinity, Salford, with some notes on the ministers, Humphrey Booth and his descendants, and the Booth charities.* [Salford]: [the church?], 1966. Includes list of ministers, and pedigree of Booth, 18-20th c.

Salford Hundred

'Particulars of the church livings in Salford Hundred, *temp* 1654', *Local notes and queries from the Manchester Guardian* **11**, 1874, 1-2.

Stalmine

FISHWICK, HENRY. 'Stalmine church and its curates', *P.N.* **2**, 1882, 244-6.

Standish

FISHER, WILLIAM FREDERICK. 'Notes on the parish church of St. Wilfred, Standish', *H.S.L.C.* **55-6**; N.S., **19-20**, 1903-4, 238-86. Includes biographical notes on rectors, 13-19th c., list of 'popish recusants', 1706, *etc.*

TEMPEST, ARTHUR CECIL, MRS. 'Some further notes on Standish church and its charities', *H.S.L.C.* **58**; N.S., **22**, 1906, 4163. Includes rate for rebuilding the church, 1582; many names.

Urswick

POSTLETHWAITE, T.N. *Some notes on Urswick church and parish: with extracts from old church books and a list of briefs, some hitherto unnoted.* Ulverston: Atkinson, 1906. Includes list of churchwardens, *etc.*

Warrington

BEAMONT, WILLIAM. *Warrington church notes: the parish church of St. Elfin, Warrington, and the other churches of the parish.* Warrington: Percival Pearse, 1878. Include biographical notes on clergy, *etc.*

RYLANDS, J. PAUL. 'Warrington in 1580: the Easter roll of moneys due to the Rector of Warrington in the twenty-second year of the reign of Queen Elizabeth', *H.S.L.C.* **55-6**; N.S., **1920**, 1903-4, 287-325. Lists 548 persons.

Warrington Deanery

'Visitation of Warrington Deanery by the Bishop of Chester in the year 1592', *H.S.L.C.* **46**; N.S., **10**, 1894, 183-92. Includes names of persons sentenced.

Warton

FLOYER J. KESTELL. 'The old rectory house and rectory of Warton' *H.S.L.C.* **57**; N.S., **21**, 1905, 28-47. Includes list of rectors, 12-20th c.

Whalley

COOKE, ALICE M., ed. *Act book of the ecclesiastical court of Whalley, 1510-1538.* C.S., N.S., **44**. 1901. For the peculiar jurisdiction of Whalley Abbey, covering the old parish of Whalley.

RAINES, F.R., ed. 'The Easter rolls of Whalley, in the years 1552 and 1553', *Chetham miscellanies* **5**. C.S., O.S., **96**. 1875, separately paginated. Lists Easter dues paid by parishioners.

Wigan

BRIDGEMAN, GEORGE T.O. *History of the church and manor of Wigan in the County of Lancaster.* C.S., N.S., **15-18**. 1888-90. Includes biographies of clergy, tithe accounts, 1616 and 1627, monumental inscriptions, *etc.*

TRUE, W.J. *A ramble round the Wigan parish church,* ed. Edgar Rodgers. Wigan: Thos. Wall and Sons, 1901. Mainly memorials, also lists of clergy and churchwardens.

B. *Baptists*

SELLARS, IAN, ed. *Our heritage: the Baptists of Yorkshire, Lancashire and Cheshire, 1647-1787-1887-1987.* Leeds: Yorkshire Baptist Association, 1987.

STOCKWELL, ARTHUR H. *The Baptist churches of Lancashire.* A.H.Stockwell, [191-]?

WHITELEY, W.T. *Baptists of North-West England, 1649-1913.* Kingsgate Press, 1913. Includes notes on 'careers of the churches'; many names.

Accrington

WYLIE, R.J.V. *The Baptist churches of Accrington and district, their formation & gradual development, with numerous character sketches of Baptist worthies.* Accrington: W. Shuttleworth, 1923. Includes extracts from baptismal records.

Hawkshead

MARTIN, JANET D. 'The Hawkshead connexion: some Cumbrian Baptists', *C.W.A.A.S.Tr.* N.S., **91**, 1991, 213-35. Includes pedigrees, 17-19th c., of Atkinson, Coulthred, Dixon, Drinkall, Grigg, Kirkby, Pritt, and Wilson.

Hill Cliff

KNOTT, O. 'Early documents relating to Hill Cliff, Warrington', *Transactions of the Baptist Historical Society* **5**, 1916-17, 154-68. Genealogical notes on various Baptist families.

Rossendale

TODD, ANDREW. 'Baptists in Rossendale', *L.* **6**(1), 1985, 613. See also **6**(2), 1985, 14-16. Includes list of churches and records; also notes on the Pickup family, 18-19th c.

C. Congregationalists, Independents, Presbyterians, and Unitarians

It is often difficult to determine which of these denominations a particular church belonged to in the seventeenth century, and they are therefore treated here together. The Unitarians were originally Presbyterian. For a general survey of the older nonconformist churches in Lancashire, see:

NIGHTINGALE, BENJAMIN. *Lancashire nonconformity, or sketches historical and descriptive of the Congregational and old Presbyterian churches in the county.* 6 vols. Manchester: John Heywood, 1890-93. v. 1. Preston, North Lancashire and Westmorland. v. 2. Blackburn District. v. 3. Bolton, Bury, Rochdale, etc. v. 4. Wigan, Warrington, St. Helens, etc. v. 5. Manchester, Oldham, Ashton, etc. v. 6. Southport, Liverpool, and the Isle of Man.

For the records of these denominations in Liverpool, see:

SMITH, JANET. 'Congregational, Presbyterian, Baptist and Unitarian records, Liverpool City Libraries, Record Office & Local History Department', *L.F.H.* **7**(3), 1985, 49-52.

The nonconformist churches grew out of the Puritanism of the Civil War years. A number of works provide important calendars of archival materials giving names *etc.* of puritan ministers in the mid-seventeeth century:

SHAW, W.A., ed. *Minutes of the Committee for the Relief of Plundered Ministers and of the Trustees for the Maintainance of Ministers, relating to Lancashire and Cheshire, 1643-1660.* L.C.R.S. **28 & 43**. 1893-96. Pt. 1. 1643-54. Pt. 2. 1650-60.

SHAW, WILLIAM A., ed. *Minutes of the Manchester Presbyterian classis.* C.S., N.S., **20, 22 & 24**. 1890-91. Gives names of ministers 1646-1660, with a few brief pedigrees.

SHAW, W.A. *Materials for an account of the Provincial Synod of the County of Lancashire, 1646-1660.* Manchester: Manchester Press, 1890. Many names of clergy.

There are a variety of miscellaneous works of use to genealogists on the subsequent history of the 'old dissent':

FISHER, HENRY, ed. *The note-book of the Rev. Thomas Jolly A.D. 1671-1693; extracts from the church book of Altham and Wymondhouses A.D. 1649-1725, and an account of the Jolly family of Standish, Gorton, and Altham.* C.S., N.S., **33**. 1894. Includes Jolly pedigree, 16-18th c. Jolly was a Presbyterian.

HIGSON, P.J.W. 'Some leading promoters of non-conformity and their association with Lancashire chapelries following the Revolution of 1688', *L.C.A.S.* **75-6**, 1965-6, 123-63. General account.

EVANS, GEORGE EYRE. *Record of the Provincial Assembly of Lancashire and Cheshire.* Manchester: H. Rawson and Co., 1896. Biographies of Congregational ministers.

NIGHTINGALE, BENJAMIN. *The story of the Lancashire Congregational Union, 1806-1906: centenary memorial volume.* Manchester: John Heywood, 1906. Includes a biographical note on 'men who have served', lists of church officers, *etc.*.

ROBINSON, W. GORDON. *A history of the Lancashire Congregational Union 1806-1956.* Manchester: Lancashire Congregational Union, 1955. General study.

LEA, JOHN. 'Historical source material on Congregationalism in nineteenth century Lancashire', *Journal of the United Reformed Church History Society*, 1(4), 1974, 106-12.

Blackburn

ABRAM, W.A. *A century of Independency in Blackburn, 1778-1878.* Blackburn: J.G. & J. Toulmin, 1878. Includes burial register, 1785-1878.

Bury

SHAW, WILLIAM A., ed. *Minutes of the Bury Presbyterian classes, 1647-1657.* C.S., N.S., **36 & 41**. 1896-8. Gives names of ministers *etc.* attending, with biographical notes.

Eccles

MCALPINE, IAN. 'An introduction to Nonconformist meeting house licences', *M.G.* **25**(2), 1989, 21-3. Includes list of licences for Eccles.

MCALPINE, IAN. *The Eccles Presbyterians, 1662-1765.* Monton: Monton Unitarian Church, 1986. Primarily a list of members.

Failsworth

GORDON, ALEXANDER. *Historical account of Dob Lane Chapel, Failsworth, and its schools.* Manchester: H. Rawson and Co., 1904. Includes extensive list of ministers and officers; also transcript of baptismal and burial registers, 1701-1807.

Leigh

PINK, W.D. *Leigh Congregationalism, 1805-1880.* Leigh: Chronicle Office, 1880. Includes list of preachers.

Liverpool

EVANS, GEORGE EWART. *A history of Renshaw Street Chapel and its institutions, with some account of the former chapel of Castle Hey and Benn's Garden, Liverpool.* C. Green and Son, 1887. Unitarian chapel in Liverpool, includes list of ministers and various officers; also lists of pew proprietors in 1727 and 1825, a few monumental inscriptions, and a list of sources.

ROBERTS, H.D. *Hope Street Chapel, Liverpool, and the allied nonconformity, being a history of the congregation worshipping in X meeting, 1707, Kaye Street meeting 1707, Paradise Street chapel, 1791, Hope Street church, 1849 ...* Liverpool: Liverpool Booksellers, 1909. Presbyterian, includes extracts from the baptismal register, 1709-68, and many other names.

Manchester

BAKER, THOMAS, SIR. *Memorials of a dissenting chapel, its foundation and worthies, being a sketch of the rise of nonconformity in Manchester and of the erection of the chapel in Cross Street, with notices of its ministers and trustees.* Simpkin, Marshall & Co., 1884. Includes 173 biographical sketches.

STRADLING, FRANCIS R. 'Early history of the Manchester Independent congregations', *M.G.* **20**(1), 1984, 21-3. Brief notes.

'Rolls of communicants', *M.G.* **20**(1), 1984, 37-9. Includes extracts from the roll of the Scottish Church, Manchester, mid-19th c.

Monton

AXON, ERNEST. 'Some early Monton ministers', *L.C.A.S.* **39**, 1921, 27-41. Brief biographies of 17-18th c. dissenting ministers.

MCALPINE, IAN. *The second Monton chapel, 1715-1802.* Monton: Monton Unitarian Church, 1986. Includes register of baptisms 1771-3, list of ministers, list of prominent members 1689-1725, *etc.*

Tockholes

NIGHTINGALE, BENJAMIN. *History of the Old Independent Chapel, Tockholes, near Blackburn, Lancashire, or, about two centuries and a half of nonconformity in Tockholes.* Manchester: John Heywood, 1886. Includes accounts of families connected with the church; also lives of ministers *etc.*

D. *Roman Catholics*

Roman Catholicism was strong in Lancashire, and its history has been the subject of many publications. A brief guide to Roman Catholic genealogy in the county is provided by:

MITCHINSON, A.J. 'Tracing a Roman Catholic family tree', *N.W.C.H.* **14**, 1987, 13-16.

For works on the secular clergy, see:

HILTON, J.A. 'The Lancashire secular clergy: a select critical bibliography', *N.W.C.H.* **20**, 1993, 76-7.

Catholic archives at Lancashire Record Office are discussed in:

FOLEY, B.C. 'The Lancashire Record Office and Roman Catholic records', *Catholic archives* **7**, 1987, 28-38.

'Some records of Roman Catholicism in Lancashire', *Lancashire Record Office report* 1966, 24-32.

Catholic missions and registers are listed in: GANDY, MICHAEL. *Catholic missions and registers 1700-1880, volume 5: North West England.* Whetstone: M. Gandy, 1993. Covers Cheshire, Lancashire, Cumberland, Westmorland and the Isle of Man.

There is a journal devoted to the history of Lancashire Catholicism:
North West Catholic history. Wigan: North West Catholic History Society, 1971- .

Amongst the many publications on Lancashire Catholicism, the following are most likely to be of use to genealogists. Arrangement is chronological:

BLUNDELL, F.O. *Old Catholic Lancashire.* 2 vols. Burns Oates & Washbourne, 1925-38.

LEATHERBARROW, J. STANLEY. *The Lancashire Elizabethan recusants.* C.S., N.S., **110.** 1947. General study; many names mentioned.

BROWNBILL, J. 'Lancashire recusants about 1630', *H.S.L.C.* **60**; N.S., **24,** 171-80. List of those who compounded for their estate, 1629-33.

BLACKWOOD, B.G. 'Plebeian Catholics in later Stuart Lancashire', *Northern history* **25,** 1989, 153-73.

DOTTIE, ROY G. 'The recusant riots at Childwall in May 1600: a reappraisal', *H.S.L.C.* **132,** 1983, 1-28. General discussion; some names.

ANSTRUTHER, GODFREY. 'Lancashire clergy in 1639: a recently discovered list among the Towneley papers', *Recusant history* **4,** 1957-8, 38-45. List of Catholic clergy to be approached to contribute to Charles I's 'Bishops War'.

BLACKWOOD, B. GORDON. 'Lancashire catholics, protestants and Jacobites', *Recusant history* **22**(1), 1994, 41-59. Includes list of Catholic gentry in 1642-8 and 1715.

'Lancashire recusants and Quakers', *H.S.L.C.* **64**; N.S., **28,** 1912, 309-19. List, 1666, of those who did not repair to their parish church.

MITCHINSON, ALAN JOSEPH, ed. *The return of the Papists for the Diocese of Chester, 1705.* Wigan: North West Catholic History Society, 1986. Important.

FRANCE, R. SHARPE, ed. *The register of estates of Lancashire Papists 1717-1788.* L.R.C.S., **98, 108 & 117.** 1945-77. v. 1. 1717. v. 2. 1717. v. 3. 1717, with list of persons registered 1718-1785. All published.

WORRAL, E.S., ed. *Return of Papists, 1767: Diocese of Chester.* Occasional publications 1. Catholic Record Society, 1980. Includes Cheshire, Lancashire, Westmorland and part of Yorkshire.

PLUMB, BRIAN. *Found worthy: a biographical dictionary of the secular clergy of the Archdiocese of Liverpool (deceased) since 1850.* Warrington: the author, 1986.

Lancashire Diocesan directory and guide to the Quarant ore for 19--. Liverpool: Publishers & Advertisers Ltd., 1926-. Roman Catholic diocese. Includes clergy lists.

Bolton

LANCASTER, J.A. 'Returns of Papists for the parishes of Bolton and Deane, in the Diocese of Chester, October 1706', *N.W.C.H.* **18,** 1991, 1-6. Transcript.

Crosby

GIBSON, THOMAS ELLISON. *Crosby records: a chapter of Lancashire recusancy, containing a relation of troubles and persecutions sustained by William Blundell of Crosby Hall, Lancashire, esq., (1560-1638) and an account of an ancient burial ground for recusants, called the Harkirke, and of coins discovered there.* C.S., N.S., **12.** 1887. Includes list of burials.

Croston

HARTLEY, MARY. 'Catholics in Croston, Lancashire, 1715', *Catholic ancestor* **4**(2), 1992 80-81. Names from the Forfeited Estate Papers at the Public Record Office.

Deane
See Bolton

Harkirk

BORG, MARY. 'Harkirk' *E.C.A. journal* **2**(1), 1986, 15-17. Notes on the Catholic register, many names.

Haslingden

DUNLEAVY, JOHN. *Haslingden Catholics, 1815-1965.* Lancashire County Council Libraries & Leisure Dept., 1987.

Lancaster

BILLINGTON, RICHARD NEWMAN, & BROWNBILL, JOHN. *St. Peters, Lancaster: a history.* Sands and Co., 1910. Roman Catholic church; includes baptisms, 1784-99, marriages, 1785-98, lists of communicants, 1799-1845, names of subscribers to the building fund, 1855-61, *etc.*

Liverpool

'Records of Catholic families in Liverpool', *Catholic Ancestor* 3(4), 1991, 152-4.

Manchester

KING, DOROTHY. 'The threat of revolution', *M.G.* 26(1), 1990, 4-6. List of Manchester and Salford Catholics who affirmed their loyalty to George III, 1793.
'Manchester Catholics', *M.G.* 19(4) 1983, 109-10. List of 495 Catholics in 1793.

North Meols

GANDY, MICHAEL. 'Catholics in North Meols, Lancashire', *Catholic history* 3(5), 1991, 209-10. From the parish register 1826-37.

Osbaldestone

POPHAM, EDWARD J. *The Osbaldestone saga.* Mellor Brook: the author, 1988.
POPHAM, EDWARD J. 'The Osbaldestone saga', *E.C.A. Journal* 2(7), 1989, 151-3. Discussion of sources for Catholic families in Osbaldestone.

Preston

DUNN, JOSEPH. *Census of the Catholic congregation of Preston, 1810 and 1820,* ed. Margaret Purnell. Blackpool: Ancestral Data Publications, 1993.
WARREN, L. 'The archives of St. Ignatius' church, Preston', *N.W.C.H.* 10, 1983, 32-3.
WARREN, LEO. *Through twenty Preston guilds: the Catholic congregation of St. Wilfred's, Preston.* Preston: St. Wilfred's, 1993. Includes list of Friargate Chapel subscribers, 1815, and various lists of vocations originating in the church; also list of casualties in both world wars.

Saint Helens

BAINES, M. ELIZABETH. 'Recusancy in St. Helens before 1649', *N.W.C.H.* 1971, 1-30.

Salford

See Manchester

West Derby Hundred

GRIGSON, W.E. ed. 'Recusant roll for West Derby Hundred 1641', *H.S.L.C.* 50; N.S., 14, 1898, 231-46.
GIBSON, A. CRAIG. 'Explanation of a deed on parchment (date 1723) presented to the Society by Mr. Harrison, of Castle Street', *H.S.L.C.* 13; N.S., 1, 1861, 301-4. List of Papists exempted from a tax on their property in West Derby Hundred, 1723.

Wigan

HILTON, J.A. 'The archives of the parishes of St. John and St. Mary, Wigan', *Catholic archives* 3, 1983, 20-21.

E. *Jews*

CAVENDISH, RICHARD. 'The Cavendish collection: Manchester Jewish Museum', *History today* 44(7), 1994, 62-3.
P[EREIRA], B.R., & M[ENDOZA], J.P. *History of the Manchester congregation of Spanish and Portuguese Jews, 5633-5683 (1873-1923).* [Manchester]: [The Synagogue?], [1923?]. Supplement 1949. Includes lists of officers, and roll of honour.
WILLIAMS, BILL. *The making of Manchester Jewry 1740-1875.* Manchester: Manchester University Press, 1976. General study; useful bibliography.

F. *Methodists*

GOWLAND, D.A. *Methodist secession: the origins of Free Methodism in three Lancashire towns: Manchester, Rochdale, Liverpool.* C.S., 3rd series 26. 1979. Includes list of lay leaders, 1835, in Liverpool, Manchester and Rochdale.
The Methodist Church North Lancashire District: Methodist History Interest Group bulletin. 1985-94. Continued by: *Wesley Historical Society North Lancashire District Branch bulletin.* 1994- .

ROSE, E.A. 'Methodism in South Lancashire to 1800', *L.C.A.S.* **81**, 1982, 67-91. Includes list of chapels, *etc.*

Blackburn
SANDFORD, H.W. 'Outline of the commencement of Blackburn Methodist Circuit archives', *Wesley Historical Society North Lancashire District branch bulletin* **21**, 1995, 9-14. General discussion of the collection.

Burnley
MOORE, B. *History of Wesleyan Methodism in Burnley and East Lancashire: Burnley, Colne, Padiham, Nelson, Barnoldswick.* Burnley: Gazette, 1899. Many names.

Longsight
'Roll of honour of Longsight Wesleyan Church and Sunday School 1918', *M.G.* 23(4), 1987, 263-5.

Preston
HODGSON, J.E.G. 'Researching a chapel roll of honour', *Wesley Historical Society North Lancashire District branch bulletin* **20**, 1994, 12-16. Discussion, based on Preston records.

Rossendale
JESSOP, WILLIAM. *An account of Methodism in Rossendale and neighbourhood.* Manchester: Tubbs, Brook and Chrystall, 1880.

Trawden
'Extract from a brief history of the Trawden Wesleyan Methodist Chapel & Sunday School, 1810-1910', *L.* 5(4), 1984, 7-8. Includes many names.

G. *Moravians*
'Early admissions to the Dukinfield Moravian Church', *M.G.* Autumn 1973, 13-15. Winter 1973-4, 7-8. 18th c.

H. *Mormons*
WATSON, REX. 'Notes on sources: Mormon ancestors', *L.* 7(2), 1986, 25-6. Brief notes.

I. *Quakers*
A number of articles provide brief notes on sources for Quaker genealogy in Lancashire:
ALSTON, ROBERT. 'Notes on sources 13: early Quakers in Lancashire', *L.* 5,(3), 1984, 9-11.
'The early Quakers of East Lancashire', *Lancashire Record Office report* 1964, 27-33. Notes on sources.
ANDREWS, JOHN. S. 'The Quaker collection of the University of Lancaster Library', *M.G.* 21(1), 1985, 44-5. Brief note.
Historical works of potential interest to genealogists include:
CADBURY, HENRY J. 'First publishers of truth in Lancashire', *Friends Historical Society journal* 31 1934, 3-19. Transcript of a 17th c. record giving names.
MORGAN, NICHOLAS J. 'Lancashire Quakers and the tithe, 1660-1730', *Bulletin of the John Rylands University Library of Manchester* 70(3), 1988, 61-76. General study.
MULLET, MICHAEL, ed. *Early Lancashire Friends.* Occasional paper 5. Lancaster: Centre for North West Regional Studies, 1978. Collection of essays; includes biographical notes on early women Quakers.
NIGHTINGALE, B. *Early stages of the Quaker movement in Lancashire.* Congregational Union of England and Wales, 1921. Includes numerous extracts from records of Quarter Sessios.
'The list of the Quakers in Lancashire and Cheshire, c.1670', *M.G.* 24(3), 1988, 164-5. Reprinted from *L.G.* 1876.

Bickerstaffe
SAGAR, JOHN H. *The Bickerstaffe Quakers c.1650 to 1800.* [Ormskirk]: Ormskirk F.H.S., [198-?] Lists Quakers, with brief genealogical notes.

Bury
MUSCHAMP, ROBERT. 'The Society of Friends: Bury District in the 17th century', *L.* 7(2), 1986, 14-21.

Hackins Hey
MURPHY, JAMES. 'The Old Quaker Meeting House in Hackins Hey, Liverpool', *H.S.L.C.* 106, 1954, 79-88. Mentions many Friends.

Lancaster

MULLET, MICHAEL. 'Historical documents at Friends Meeting House, Lancaster', *Journal of the Friends Historical Society* **54**(1), 1976, 33-4. Lists records of the Meeting.

Swarthmore

GAYTHORPE, HARPER. 'Swarthmore meeting-house, Ulverston: a Quaker stronghold', *C.W.A.A.S.Tr.* N.S., **6**, 1906, 237-83. Includes names of 173 Friends interred, with many extracts from accounts, *etc.*

Tottington

COUPE, GLADYS. *The Quakers of Tottington, 1654-1682.* Swinton: Neil Richardson, 1986.

12. EDUCATIONAL SOURCES

In the last four centuries it is probable that the majority of our ancestors attended school. Educational archives record some of their names, as well as those of their teachers, and there are many publications on educatonal history which may be of genealogical value. For a useful guide to the sources, see:

PROCTER, M.R., ed. *Education on Merseyside: a guide to the sources.* Liverpool: Merseyside Archives Liaison Group, 1992.

See also:

'The archives of some Lancashire grammar schools', *Lancashire Record Office report* 1955, 12-18.

Two other general works may also be consulted:

WALLIS, P.J. *A preliminary register of old schools in Lancashire and Cheshire',* *H.S.L.C.* **120**, 1969, 1-21.

PORTEUS, T.C. *Lancashire school founders and other famous friends of Lancashire boys and girls.* Coppull: the Author, 1929. Brief biographical notes.

For Lancastrians at Cambridge colleges, see:

'Admissions at Emmanuel College, Cambridge, 1610-1723', *P.N.,* **4**, 1884, 78-81. List for Cheshire and Lancashire.

AXON, ERNEST. *Lancashire and Cheshire admissions to Gonville and Caius College, Cambridge, 1558-1678.* Manchester: L.C.A.S., 1889. Reprinted from *L.C.A.S.* **6**, 1888, 74-97.

GRIGSON, FRANCIS. 'Admissions to Jesus College, Cambridge, 1618-1719', *P.N.* **3**, 1883, 266-8. List for Cheshire and Lancashire.

For World War I servicemen from Manchester University, see:

Manchester University roll of service. Publications **146.** Manchester: University of Manchester, 1922. Includes brief biographical notes.

Abbeystead

ROPER, W.O. 'Abbeystead in Wyresdale and its endowed school', *H.S.L.C.* **55-6**; N.S., **19-20**, 1903-4, 67-89. Names many masters and trustees; also lists curates of Wyresdale from 1608.

Ashton in Makerfield

HODGKISS, W.J. 'Seneley Green Grammar School, Ashton-inMakerfield', *H.S.L.C.* **104**, 1952 1-34. General account, 16-19th c.

Blackburn

EASTWOOD, G.F. *Queen Elizabeth's: a new history of the ancient Grammar School of Blackburn.* Blackburn: The Governors, 1967.

GARSTANG, JOHN. *A history of the Blackburn Grammar School, founded A.D. 1514.* Blackburn: North East Lancashire Press Co., 1897. Includes list of masters 1514-1595.

STOCKS, GEORGE ALFRED, ed. *The records of Blackburn Grammar School.* C.S., N.S., **66-8**. 1909. Includes deeds, accounts, *etc.* 16-18th c.

Bolton

BROWN, W.E. *The history of Bolton School.* Bolton: Bolton School, 1976. Many names.

W., J.K. 'The old grammar school lads', in BARTON, B.T., ed. *Historical gleanings of Bolton and District [third series].* Bolton: Daily Chronicle Office, 1883, 362-402. Index of registers of Bolton Grammar School, 1808-55.

'Records of the Bolton Grammar School', in BARTON, B.T., ed. *Historical gleanings of Bolton and District [first series].* Bolton: Daily Chronicle Office, 1881, 366-94. Gives names of masters, trustees and others associated with the school.

Bretherton

ROSE, JANE. 'The founding of Bretherton School', in FRANCE, R. SHARPE, ed. *A Lancashire miscellany.* L.C.R.S., **109**, 1965, 1-12. Gives names of benefactors; also of opponents of the foundation.

Bury

HEWITSON, WILLIAM. 'Head masters of Bury Grammar School', *Bury and Rossendale historical review* **2**, 1910-11, 80-83 & 116-8. 17-18th c.

RAISTRITH,S.N. 'Boarding schools for girls in Bury, 1851', *L.* **1**(5), 1976, 95-7. Census listing.

Cheadle Hulme

BOWER, J. '1871 census of Manchester Warehousemen and Clerks Orphan School, Cheadle Hulme', *North Cheshire family historian* **13**(1), 1986, 9-10. Mainly lists children born in Manchester, although the school was in Cheshire.

Clitheroe

GREEN, DUDLEY, & HARWOOD, KEITH. *Queen Mary's Grammar School, Clitheroe: a history of Clitheroe Royal Grammar School, 1554-1983.* Chorley: Countryside Publications, 1983. Includes much information on headmasters.

STOKES, C.W. *Queen Mary's Grammar School, Clitheroe. Part 1. The sixteenth and seventeenth centuries.* C.S., N.S., **92**. 1934. No more published. General history, includes calendar of documents, also lists of governors, masters and ushers, and pedigrees of Aspinall, Houghton, Greenacres, Parke, Lister, and Hammerton, and of Nowell.

Coniston

'Henry Tyson's notebook Coniston School', *C.F.H.S.N.* **4**, 197, 10-11. Gives many names of school-children at Coniston *etc.* 1804-13.

Crosby

LUFT, H.M. *A history of Merchant Taylors' School, Crosby, 1620-1970.* Liverpool: Liverpool University Press, 1970. Scholarly history; many names.

RUSSELL, C.F. 'An old register of Merchant-Taylors School, Crosby', *H.S.L.C.* **96**, 1944, 70-77. Includes list of boys, 1830-43.

RUSSELL, C.F. 'Some early headmasters at Merchant Taylors' School, Great Crosby', *H.S.L.C.* **87**, 1935, 123-30. 17-18th c. Includes biographical and genealogical notes, with brief pedigrees of Ashworth and Waring.

HARROP, SYLVIA. *The Merchant Taylors' School for Girls, Crosby: one hundred years of achievement, 1888-1988.* Liverpool: University Press, 1988.

Disley

UNSWORTH, C. 'Springfield Boarding School, Flixton Road, Disley: 1881 census', *M.G.* 25(4), 1989, 66.

Droylsden

'1851 census returns: 163, Manchester Road Droylsden: Moravian establishment for needlework, staff and boarders', *M.G.* 4(3) 1968, 7.

BECKET, J.D. '1851 census returns: 182, Manchester Road, Droylsden: the Ladies Seminary', *M.G.* 4(4), 1968, 15.

'1851 census, Droylsden, Manchester: staff and pupils at Fairfield Academy', *M.G.* 4(2), 1968, 13-15.

Halliwell

'The Jubilee School, Halliwell', in BARTON, B.T., ed. *Historical gleanings of Bolton and District [first series].* Bolton: Daily Chronicle Office, 1881, 288-95. Includes list of subscribers, 1809.

Lancaster

MURRAY, ATHOL, ed. *A biographical register of the Royal Grammar School, Lancaster.* 2 vols. Cambridge: W.Heffer & Sons, 1962. Pt. 1. From the 17th century to 1859. Pt. 2. From 1850 to 1872.

RANDLES, R.H.S. *History of the Friends School, Lancaster.* Lancaster: Allan Sharpe, 1982. Includes various lists of names, 18-20th c.

The Castle Howell School record, comprising a list of pupils from the beginning, papers on the origin, name and changes, by principals, and miscellaneous articles contributed by old boys. Lancaster: R. & G. Brash, 1888. A Lancaster school.

Leigh

LUNN, JOHN. *A history of Leigh Grammar School (Lancashire), 1592-1932.* Manchester: Sherratt & Hughes, 1935. Includes various lists of names.

Liverpool

'Liverpool schools records in Liverpool Record Office', *L.F.H.S.J.* 1(3), 1977, 57-9. List of archives.

MURPHY, JAMES. 'The rise of public elementary education in Liverpool', *H.S.L.C.* 116, 1964, 167-95; 118, 1966, 105-38. Pt. 1. 1784-1818. Pt. 2. 1819-35. Includes list of schools.

BROWN, A.T. *Some account of the Royal Institution School, Liverpool, with a roll of masters and boys (1819-1892 A.D.).* 2nd ed. Liverpool: University Press, 1927.

HUGHES, JOHN R. 'A sketch of the origin and early history of the Liverpool Blue Coat Hospital', *H.S.L.C.* 11, 1859, 163-86; 12, N.S., 1, 1861, 71-102; 16; N.S., 4, 1888, 57-78. Includes list of subscribers, 1709, and of fifty trustees elected 1803.

ORMEROD, HENRY A. *The Liverpool Free School. (1515-1803).* Liverpool: University Press, 1951. Includes list of masters.

MCCANN, JO. 'Orphans (?) in Liverpool', *L.F.H.* 15(3), 1993, 68-72. Includes transcript of 1861 and 1871 census of St. Elizabeth's Certified Industrial School, 22, Soho Street, Liverpool.

1888 to 1912 A.D: Greenbank School, Liverpool: a memoir, with a scroll of masters, mistresses and boys. Liverpool: University Press of Liverpool, 1939.

Liverpool College boys and the European War, 1914-1915. [Liverpool?]: [ ], 1915. List of soldiers, including photographs.

Manchester

BAILEY, JOHN EGLINGTON. 'Former masters of the Manchester Grammar School', *L.C.A.S.* 3, 1885, 134-43. 16-17th c.

GRAHAM, J.A., & PHYTHIAN, B.A., eds. *The Manchester Grammar School, 1515-1965.* Manchester: Manchester University Press, 1965. Includes list of high masters.

HIBBERT, S. *History of the foundations in Manchester of Christ's College, Chethams Hospital, and the Free Grammar School.* 2 vols. William Pickering, 1834. Extensive.

MUMFORD, ALFRED A. *The Manchester Grammar School, 1515-1915: a regional study of the advancement of learning in Manchester since the Reformation.* Longmans Green and Co., 1919. Extensive.

MANCHESTER GRAMMAR SCHOOL. *A biographical register of old Mancunians, 1888-1951.* Manchester: The School, 1965.

MANCHESTER GRAMMAR SCHOOL. *A biographical register of old Mancunians, 1914-1965 (including amendments for pre-1914).* 2nd ed. Manchester: [The School], 1978.

POLLARD, MARJORIE. 'Chetham's Hospital', *M.G.* 26(4), 1990, 7-9. Lists first pupils 1653, new admissions in 1799 and apprentices, 1813-15.

SMITH, JEREMIAH FINCH, ed. *The admission register of the Manchester School, with some notices of the more distinguished scholars.* C.S., O.S., **69, 73, 93 & 94.** 1866-74. v. 1. 1730-1775. v.2. 1776-1807. v. 3. 1807-1837 (2 pts.)

WHATTON, WILLIAM ROBERT. *The history of Manchester School, comprising the foundation, the original charters and statutes and the revenues and expenditure; also an account of the exhibitions and scholarships, with lists of those persons who have enjoyed the various allowances to the universities, and the nomination of the feoffees and high masters, illustrated by numerous biographical and explanatory notes,*
and a memoir of the life of the founder. William Pickering, 1834. Extensive.

'Chetham Blue Coat School, 1851 census, Manchester', *M.G.* 20(1), 1984, 5-6.

BURNEY, LESTER. *Cross Street Chapel schools, Manchester, 1734-1942.* Didsbury: Peter C. Woolley, 1977. Many names, but unfortunately no index.

KENNEDY, MICHAEL. *The history of the Royal Manchester College of Music, 1893-1972.* Manchester: Manchester University Press, 1971. Includes list of officers, honorary fellows, and scholarships and prize winners.

LEVER, H., & BIRKBY, J.G. *A short history of the Central High School for Boys, Manchester.* [ ], [193-?]. Includes list of past and present staff.

THOMPSON, JOSEPH. *The Owen's College: its foundation and growth, and its connection with the Victoria University, Manchester.* Manchester: J.E. Cornish, 1886. Includes lists of governors, teaching staff, and benefactors.

'Are your ancestors listed here? The pupils of Joseph Hobhouse, at Manchester in 1725', *M.G.* 4(1), 1968, 6-8.

'Ladies Jubliee School', *M.G.* 25(1), 1989, 9-10. 1851 census for 25, New Bridge Street, Manchester.

Roll of students entered at the Manchester Academy, 1786-1803; Manchester College, York, 1803-1840, Manchester New College, Manchester, 1840-1853, Manchester New College, London, 1853-1867; with a list of the professors and principal officers. Manchester: Johnson and Rawson, 1868.

Miles Platting

WINSTANLEY, DAVID. *A schoolmaster's notebook, being an account of a nineteenth century experiment in social welfare,* ed. Edith and Thomas Kelly. C.S., 3rd series **8.** 1957. Concerns education and social reform in Miles Platting; includes list of hand loom weavers, 1835, list of Sir Benjamin Heywood's tenants, 1840, *etc.*

Newton

'A Lancashire charity school', *Lancashire Record Office report* 1966 38-47. Records of Blue Coat School at Newton with Scales, Kirkham.

North Meols

AUGHTON, PETER. 'North Meols Sunday School, 1814', *L.F.H.* 4(3), 1982, 55-6. List of scholars.

Ormskirk

BATE, J.R. 'Ormskirk Grammar School: the first minute book, 1613-1890', *H.S.L.C.* **76; N.S., 40,** 1925, 91-114. Discussion; some names.

ORRITT, DAVID C.J. *The history of Ormskirk Grammar School, Lancashire.* Preston: Carnegie Press, 1988. Includes lists of names.

Penketh

HODGSON, JOSEPH SPENCE. *A history of Penketh School 1834-1907, with the addition of a list of teachers and officers and a list of scholars.* Headley Brothers for the Penketh Old Scholars Association, 1907.

Poulton le Fylde

PAGETT, ARTHUR C. *A history of Baine's Grammar School.* Worcester: Privately published, 1928. At Poulton le Fylde.

Rivington

KAY, MARGARET M. *The history of Rivington and Black Rod Grammar School.* Manchester: Manchester University Press, 1931. Includes a list of scholars, 1575, names of governors, 16-18th c., list of primary sources *etc.*

Rossall

BENNETT, PETER. *A very desolate position: the story of the birth and development of a Victorian public school.* [Fleetwood]: Rossall Archives, 1977. Includes information on the masters of Rossall School.

ROWBOTHAM, JOHN FREDERICK. *The history of Rossall School.* 2nd ed. Manchester: John Heywood, 1901. Includes list of assistant masters, 1831-92 *etc.*

FURNEAUX, L.R. *Floreat Rossallia: Rossall school register, 1844-1923.* 6th ed. Godalming: [ ], [1923].

The Rossall School register: seventh edition, 1871-1939. Cambridge University Press for the School, 1940.

M., J.R.F. *The Rossall School register; eighth edition, 1881-1954* Spottiswoode, Ballantyne & Co., for the School, 1956. Includes lists of all boys from 1844.

GRAHAM, M.A. *The Rossall School register ... 1910-1967.* 9th ed. Rossall: the School, 1968.

Stonyhurst

MUIR, T.E. *Stonyhurst College 1593-1993.* James & James, 1992. Includes brief notes on a few prominent old boys of this Roman Catholic school; also a 'select bibliography'.

GERARD, JOHN. *Centenary record: Stonyhurst College: its life beyond the seas 1592-1794, and on English soil, 1794-1894.* Belfast: Marcus Ward & Co. 1894. Includes descent of Stonyhurst Hall, medieval-18th c.

IRWIN, FRANCIS. *Stonyhurst war record: a memorial of the part taken by Stonyhurst men in the Great War.* Stonyhurst: Stonyhurst College, 1927.

Tottington

COUPE, GLADYS. *The three r's in Tottington before 1870.* Swinton: Neil Richardson, 1989.

Upholland

BAGLEY, J.J. *Upholland Grammar School: the evolution of a school through three centuries.* Liverpool: University Press of Liverpool, 1944. Includes list of headmasters, and bibliography.

BAGLEY, J.J. 'The foundation and financing of Upholland Grammar School', *H.S.L.C.* **101**, 1949, 85-96. Includes folded pedigree of Molyneaux and Leigh, 17-18th c., pedigree of Bispham 17th c. and a list of 'schoole stocke and wages paid by the inhabitants of Holland, Orrell, and Winstanley', 1673, *etc.*

Warrington

BOWES, JOHN. 'The origin and history of the Warrington Blue Coat School', *H.S.L.C.* **22**; N.S., **10**, 1870, 89-126. Includes names of some trustees and teachers, 17-19th c., list of benefactors, 17th c., notes on Patten, Blackburne and Lyon families, and list of thirty pupils, 1782, *etc.*

O'BRIEN, P. *Warrington Academy 1757-86: its predecessors and successors.* Wigan: Owl Books, 1989. Extensive general history.

MCLACHLAN, W.H. *Warrington Academy: its history and influence.* C.S., N.S., **107**. 1943. General history of an 18th c. nonconformist academy. Mentions many names.

Whalley

FIELD, FLORENCE A., & BIRDSALL, G.B. *The coming of age souvenir of the Whalley Range High School.* Sherratt & Hughes, 1912. Includes 'Old girls directory.'

Wigan

CHAMBRES, GORDON CREWE. *History of Wigan Free Grammar School, 1596-1869, together with an account of the Sherington family of Wigan.* 2nd ed. Wigan: Thos. Wall & Sons, 1937.

HAWKES, ARTHUR JOHN. *Wigan Grammar School 1596-1936: an historical and biographical retrospect.* Wigan: The Author, 1937.

13. MIGRATION

Lancashire has witnessed the comings and goings of many people, some of whom have left traces behind them. Industrialisation attracted numerous immigrants, especially the Irish; conversely many Lancastrians have migrated. A number of brief miscellaneous articles on migration to Lancashire are available:

CROSS, ALAN G. 'Migration to Preston in the fourteenth century: the evidence of surnames', *Lancashire local historian* **8**, 1993, 6-17.

SMITH, JOHN H. 'The North-West: magnet for migrants, 1750-1914', *M.G.* **28**(1), 1992, 65-75. General.

POOLEY, COLIN G. & TURNBULL, JEAN. 'Migration in North West England from 1750 to the present day', *M.G.* **30**(4), 1994, 1519. Discussion of a research project at Lancaster University.

WYATT, GRACE. 'Migration in South-West Lancashire: a study of three parishes', *Local population studies* **27**, 1981, 62-4. Based on the parish registers of Halsall, Sefton and Aughton, 1661-1760. Brief.

German miners at Coniston formed a distinct community in the seventeenth century:

COLLINGWOOD, W.G. 'Germans at Coniston in the seventeenth century', *C.W.A.A.S.Tr.* N.S., **10** 1910, 369-94. Biographical notes on 85 individuals.

Irish, and, to a lesser degree, Scottish migrants have played a major role in Lancashire history, especially in Liverpool and Manchester. A number of works on them are available; the following is a very select listing.

NEAL, FRANK. *Sectarian violence: the Liverpool experience 1819-1914: an aspect of Anglo-Irish history.* Manchester University Press, 1988.

PROCTER, MARGARET. *The Irish community in North-West England: a guide to local archive sources.* Liverpool: Merseyside Record Office - Institute of Irish Studies, 1993.

BECKETT, J.D, ed. *A dictionary of Scottish emigrants into England & Wales.* Manchester: M.L.F.H.S., 1988. Includes many immigrants to Lancashire.

WHYTE, IAN. 'Invisible immigrants: the migration of Scots to Manchester in the eighteenth and nineteenth centuries', *M.G.* **27**(4), 1991, 48-54. General study.

Many migrants also came to Lancashire from other parts of England, especially as a consequence of the Poor Law migration scheme. A number of articles on this topic are available; reference should also made to the works listed under the heading 'Apprentices' in section 5 above.

BENTON, TONY. 'Here is a living ... and a good one: movement to Lancashire and Cheshire under the 1835-7 sponsored Poor Law migration scheme', *L.* **7**(1), 1986, 30-33.

TODD, ANDREW A. 'Notes on sources, 16: the 1843 return of sponsored Poor Law migrants', *L.* **6**(2), 1985, 28-32. General discussion, includes pedigree of Bacon, of Soham Fen and Rossendale.

PRYER, WALTER. 'The Bledlow migrants to the North', *Origins: magazine of the Buckinghamshire Family History Society* **7**(3), 1983, 114-5. Extracts from Lancashire and Cheshire census returns relating to Buckinghamshire migrants.

REES, CATHERINE. 'The sponsored Poor Law migration scheme, 1835-1837, a study of the Preston area', *Lancashire local historian* **6** 1991, 23-31. Study of in-migration, includes extracts from 1841 census for Preston, Penwortham and Walton-LeDale.

'Suffolk paupers', *Suffolk roots* **7**(3), 1981, 40-41. Lists paupers assisted to migrate from Suffolk to Lancashire and other northern counties, 1836.

PARK, P.B. *An index to Cumbrians in Liverpool.* 4 vols. [ ]: Cumbria F.H.S., 1986-92.

For the migration of Lancastrians overseas, see:

MORLEY, D.J. 'Lancashire people in first census of Western Australia, 1832', *M.G.* **18**(1), 1982, 5-6.

COHEN, I. 'American management and British labor: Lancashire immigrant spinners in industrial New England', *Comparative studies in society and history* **27**(4), 1985, 608-50. General discussion; includes bibliography.

'Lancashire', in COLDHAM, PETER WILSON. *Bonded passengers to America, volume VIII: Northern Circuit, 1665-1775.* Baltimore: Genealogical Publishing Co., 1983, 14-19.

ELTON, JOHN. 'Liverpool lists of emigrants to America 1697-1706', *H.S.L.C.* **53**; N.S., **17**, 1901, 179-88. Includes list of servants emigrating on the *Loyalty,* 1698.

TAYLOR, BETTY. 'Liverpool list of emigrants', *North Cheshire family historian* **18**(1), 1991, 30-31. List of servant who sailed to Virginia on the *Liberty*, 1698.

FRANCE, R. SHARPE. 'Early emigrants to America from Liverpool', *Genealogists' magazine* **12**(7), 1956, 234-5.

Family Name Index

Place Name Index

94

Author Index